HIJRA

STORY AND SIGNIFICANCE

ZAKARIA BASHIER

THE ISLAMIC FOUNDATION

Published by

THE ISLAMIC FOUNDATION

Markfield Conference Centre
Ratby Lane, Markfield
Leicestershire, LE67 9SY, United Kingdom
Tel: +44 (0)1530 244944/5, Fax: +44 (0)1530 244946
E-mail: publications@islamic-foundation.org.uk
Website: www.islamic-foundation.org.uk

Distributed by Kube Publishing Ltd.

Quran House, P.O.Box 30611, Nairobi, Kenya

P.M.B. 3193, Kano, Nigeria

1st Reprint 1987/1407 H.
2nd Reprint 2002/1423 H.
3rd Reprint 2007/1428 H.

British Library Cataloguing-in-Publication Data
Bashier, Zakaria
Hijra
1. Muhammad (*Prophet*) – Biography
2. Muslims – Saudi Arabia – Biography
I. Title
297'.63 BP75

Printed and bound in England by Antony Rowe Ltd, Chippenham, Wiltshire

ISBN 9780860371243 Pbk

بسم الله الرحمن الرحيم

Contents

ARABIC WORDS AND NAMES

A few words about how Arabic words and names have been typeset in English.

1 Some words have been neither italicised nor given accents; they are now frequently used and have become commonly known, and should therefore become part of the English language, as have become Islam and Muslim, like:

Allah; Muhammad; Ahmad; ‘Abdullah; ‘Ali; Sunnah; Hadith; Ummah; Hijra; Jihad; Da‘wah; Masjid; Imam; Muezzin; Qur’an; Surah; Qibla; Sunni; Shi‘a; Ulama.

2 Some words, because they are frequently used in the book, have been italicised and given accents when they appear for the first time in the text, but are not italicised nor given accents subsequently, like:

Muhājir/s, Ansari/Anṣār, Adhān, Munāfiq, Kāfir, Sharī‘ah, Dār al-Islām, Dār al-Ḥarb.

3 English equivalents of the key Islamic term have their first letter capitalised, like:

Prayer, Fasting, Almsgiving, Pilgrimage, Messenger, Mosque, Hereafter.

4 Proper names have been given accents to help with their correct pronunciation, but not italicised.

Preface

The Hijra is both an event and a symbol. The physical journey from Makka to Madina symbolises the eternal imperative of Islam – surrender to One God alone – to make the culture, the society, the environment, *Muslim* to Him, just as the individual. Towards this end a Muslim must always ceaselessly strive.

There have always been many Muslims who find themselves, for diverse reasons, living in predominantly non-Muslim communities, but in a world shrunken by modern communications, this is in a sense the situation of *all* Muslims today. The continuing economic and military supremacy of the Western countries (however sterile the cultural foundations of this supremacy may have become) makes of the whole world a predominantly non-Muslim community, in which it is more and more difficult to retain a sure grasp of Muslim ideals and culture – whether for the individual or for the state. In this moving account of the Muslim exodus from non-Muslim Makka to Madina, and in the subsequent analysis of it, my brother Dr. Zakaria Bashier offers an instructive parallel to the situation of the modern Muslim. This is a story of endurance and triumph in the face of seemingly insuperable adversity; it tells of idealism and courageous faith in the possibility of a just and free Islamic state, and of the setting-up of such a state under the authority of the Prophet Muhammad, upon him be peace. But as well as being an historical event, the Hijra is a symbolic one – Dr. Bashier argues for the rebuilding of a fully aware Muslim consciousness that can stand firm against the temptations of facile compromise and half-hearted commitment, and visualise, once more, a truly independent Islamic community, confident of its traditions and its ideals.

Dr. Bashier's book, therefore, meets a great need at a time when Muslims stand on the threshold of the fifteenth century after the Hijra. I am convinced that his treatment will enlighten many minds and inspire many hearts to pursue the ideals that the Hijra encompasses. I am grateful to him for having written a very timely work. I also acknowledge the valuable assistance provided by Dr. Jamil Qureshi in the editing of this book.

May Allah bless our humble efforts with His acceptance, grace and forgiveness.

Islamic Foundation,
Leicester
1st April, 1983

Khurram Murad
Director General

Part One

THE HIJRA

1

The Order to Migrate

PROLOGUE

The death of Abū Ṭālib left the Prophet without a protecting ally, and the death of Khadījah without personal moral support, in a Makka that refused his call to Islam. His attempt to find a new base in Taif had been frustrated. Yemen and Abyssinia were too far away and were not, for other reasons besides, suitable places in which to establish a Muslim community under the Prophet's leadership. He was, it is true, offered the guarantee of Muṭ'im ibn 'Uday which was temporarily sufficient; but it did not, in a hostile Makka, afford security – either for the Prophet's own person or for the Muslims – such as they had enjoyed from Abū Ṭālib. The polytheists of Makka were not slow to realise the significance of Abū Ṭālib's death and intensified their persecution. Darkness threatened to extinguish the new faith, and the chances of survival for the nascent Muslim community seemed slim indeed. Now, when all other avenues were closed, hope came from the direction of Yathrib. It was to this ancient Arabian oasis in the North that, after his return from Taif, the Prophet's thoughts turned. Here, in contrast to Makka, the birth of Islam and the events it had provoked had caused a favourable stir. The interest in Islam grew in Yathrib and very quickly assumed the proportions of a movement which culminated in the conclusion of the two 'Aqaba pledges. The second 'Aqaba pledge promised not only a refuge but, more significantly,[1] political alliance and military defence of the Islamic cause.

There were grounds then, both negative and positive, for the Hijra. The Makkans were not passive in their refusal of

[1] For a discussion of the full meaning of the second 'Aqaba pledge (the Pledge of War) see pp. 98-9.

Islam; they sought feverishly to eradicate it. Muslims had no security nor rights in Makka – their lives were under threat and their property fair game to usurpers. The Prophet, upon him be peace, had no choice but to seek an alternative environment – Makka was barren, incapable of bearing the fruits of his Prophetic mission. On the positive side were the good hopes and generous prospects opened up by the second 'Aqaba pledge.

Until about this time, the Muslims had been forbidden to fight, even in self-defence. The Prophet ordered them to endure harassment and persecution with patience and courage, to meet the intransigence of the Quraysh with peaceful resistance. This was indeed the best policy. Fighting was, perhaps, impracticable – since the company of Muslims did not exceed one hundred, they were hopelessly outmatched in numbers and arms by the Quraysh. But it was also a matter of paramount importance that the Muslims did not jeopardise even the remote hope of peaceful co-existence in Makka by resorting to armed defence. Such peace as there was could be used to spread the message of Islam. Also, as Islam is a religion that strongly emphasises the use of reason and valid arguments to win converts, it is only to be expected that it urged its adherents to peace. There was to be no compulsion in religion and the new faith needed time to spread its ideas through persuasion. Had the first Muslims been too ready to engage in conflict, the opportunities to disseminate Islam peacefully would have been tragically lessened, perhaps even wholly lost. Furthermore, the Prophet Muhammad, upon him be peace, and his Companions were firm in their faith that Islam is the revealed word of God; that it is the only and ultimate truth; that its ideas hold the greatest promise of deliverance and liberation for mankind; that these ideas were also particularly relevant to the Arabian environment, then in a state of social chaos; that, indeed, for the whole world of that time Islam was an idea whose hour had come. In short, the Muslims were confident that, as an idea, Islam could not be conquered by the strongest armies, nor needed an army to spread its teachings.

A military confrontation with the Quraysh, while in Makka whose outcome might have favoured the Quraysh, could not have served any useful end, and had to be averted by every means possible. A confrontation under the civil authority of the Quraysh would have appeared as nothing more than a civil disorder, and interpreted as such by neutral observers on the Makkan scene, those as yet uncommitted and undecided. Any attempt by those early Muslims to strike back at the Quraysh was certain to have been viewed as anarchical, as deliberately sowing the seeds of social strife and dissension within the Makkan community. That would, in turn, have alienated the undecided minds, whose conversion to Islam was to be hoped for. In addition to all this, it was by no means lost upon the Prophet, upon him be peace, that he was engaged with the Quraysh in a propaganda war in which they (being well established in Arabia and owning unquestioned authority and prestige) naturally had a big advantage. Their commercial caravans frequently journeyed north and south spreading the Qurayshite version of what was happening in Makka, including their view of the Prophet's movement. But, however much they lied about him and his message, they could not make things happen that did not in fact happen. That the Prophet, upon him be peace, fully recognised this propaganda war as such, is amply attested by a later incident involving the chief of the Hypocrites in Madina, 'Abdullah ibn Ubayy: when the Muslims, led by the Prophet himself, were returning from the expedition of Banū al-Musṭalaq (6 AH), a vicious petty quarrel broke out between one of the *Anṣār* (the native supporters) and one of the *Muhājirs* (emigrants), and threatened to develop into a serious conflict between the two Muslim groups. 'Abdullah ibn Ubayy is reported to have tried his best to add fuel to this flare-up. He said that when they returned to Madina, the stronger (meaning the Ansar) would drive out the weaker (meaning the Muhajirs). When this became known, the Prophet, upon him be peace, was advised by some of his senior Companions to kill 'Abdullah ibn Ubayy for his proven treason. But the Prophet promptly replied that he would not have the Arabs (Quraysh) passing the word around that Muhammad killed his followers.

Thus, in the circumstances that prevailed up to the time of the Hijra, peaceful resistance to the oppression by the Quraysh was the best course for the Muslims: the Prophet, upon him be peace, would urge his persecuted Companions to bear their afflictions with patience, assure them that they would be rewarded by God in the Hereafter, and God would find a way out for them. Facing persecution with patience strengthened their faith and resolve. There was nothing much he need do to alleviate their suffering other than profound supplications to his Lord for their deliverance from their enemies and the ultimate victory of the Muslim cause.

GOD'S PERMISSION TO WAGE WAR

When it became evident that the Quraysh's aggressive persecution of Muslims would observe no restraint, God revealed to the Prophet that it was henceforth permissible to fight the unbelievers in self-defence. Ibn Hishām states:

> The Apostle of God, upon him be peace, had not been given permission to fight or shed blood before the second 'Aqaba pledge. He was simply commanded to call men to God, and to bear injury and insult, forgiving the crude and the insolent.

The Quraysh had persecuted the Prophet's followers, tried to tempt some from their religion, and banished others. The Muslims were compelled either to reject Islam or, if they would not, to continue to endure oppression and maltreatment, or else to emigrate – some to Abyssinia, some to Madina, and some elsewhere.

When the Quraysh thus transgressed against God, rejecting what was designed for them of honour and dignity (if they accepted Islam), when they belied His Apostle and maltreated those who worshipped God Alone, God gave His permission to fight back in self-defence. 'Urwah ibn al-Zubayr and other men of learning have said that the following Qur'ānic verse was revealed in this connection:

> Permission to wage war in self-defence is given to those who have been fought against because they were wronged. God is able to help them. Those who were expelled from their homes without right, only because they said 'God alone is our Lord'. Had not God driven back some groups of people, those by means of others, monasteries and churches, synagogues and mosques, wherein the name of God is much remembered,

> would have been destroyed. Assuredly God will give victory to those who give victory to Him – assuredly God is All-Strong, All-Mighty – (Assuredly He will give victory to those) who, if We establish them in the land, perform prayer and pay the *Zakāt,* enjoin righteousness and forbid lewdness. And to God belongs the sequel of all matters. (al-Ḥajj, 22: 39-41)

Then Ibn Hishām adds:

> Then Allah said: 'Fight them so that there will not be persecution (because of religion) and the religion will be God's alone'. (al-Baqarah, 2: 98)

The above verse makes it very clear that fighting was sanctioned in Islam insofar as it was deemed an indispensable means of self-defence for a peaceful and righteous Muslim group subjected to the worst temptation and persecution because of their worship of the one true God. Self-defence assumes the status of a holy obligation when a worthy cause is imperilled – in the case of those early Muslims, the cause was their right to worship God and proclaim His mission to mankind. Persecution of a peaceful monotheistic minority because of their steadfastness in their conviction is indeed an act of war; it is viewed by the Qur'ān as worse than killing and justifying retaliation. Persecution because of religious conviction should be combated by force, if necessary, 'so that all religion will be God's alone'.

This principle must be upheld by Muslims even if they are not directly affected by the religious oppression and persecution. Tyranny over the minds and hearts of men is a cardinal evil which operates like a cancer in the human community, and is bound – if permitted to grow unchecked in one environment – to spread everywhere and affect everybody. Thus Muslims cannot stand by while it is practised in their neighbourhood. If Muslims fail to see the importance of combating tyranny and oppression when it is practised next door, they will pay dearly for it: in due course, their own freedom of worship may be utterly denied to them, and no house of God will be spared from destruction, be it Jewish, Christian or Muslim. Perhaps this verse is the clearest Qur'ānic injunction to monotheistic believers to unite in opposing religious persecution, if they want to preserve their religious liberties. This injunction is clearly implied in the allusion to 'monasteries and churches, synagogues and mosques'.

According to the Qur'ānic verse above, it is especially when persecution extends to driving people out of their homes that fighting becomes an urgent and unavoidable imperative. The allusion to the expulsion of people from their homes indicates that at the time when this verse was revealed, the exodus to Madina had already begun. This seems an inescapable conclusion since, up to the time of the second 'Aqaba pledge, fighting was not permitted. This is confirmed by the Prophet's reply to the Yathribites who, after undertaking the second 'Aqaba pledge, asked to raid the Quraysh's quarters. He told them that he had no orders to fight.

It would be a misreading of the position of those early Muslims to consider that they had submitted passively to the maltreatment and oppression of the Quraysh without a clear understanding of their position, or some plans for the future. It would be equally wrong to think that Islam is a religion that advocates letting wrongdoers go unchecked. Rather, it is a distinctive characteristic of the early Muslims that they never let the wrong go unchallenged. This characteristic is sanctioned and praised by the Qur'ān.:

> ... and what is with God is better and more lasting for those who believe and put their trust in their Lord. And those who avoid major sins and lewdness, and who when they are angry, forgive. And those who answer the call of their Lord, perform the prayer, and their affairs are a matter of counsel amongst them, and who spend of what We have bestowed upon them. And those who, when injustice is done to them, help and defend themselves. (al-Shūrā, 42: 36-39)

If the Muslims did not retaliate against the insolence of the Quraysh, it was because the Prophet forbade it, who knew the quality of faith that has suffered and survived harsh trial. To resist and contain the oppression led by the Quraysh would need Muslims of that quality, prepared to battle not for revenge but for right: spiritual readiness was the first essential. Secondly, to engage in armed resistance would have been pointless until the objective conditions for it existed – namely, a defensible territory, that was adequate in both human and natural resources; a community, committed and dedicated to Islamic ideals; and a strong and effective Muslim political authority. These conditions had to be fulfilled before the Muslims could hope to undertake a successful war of self-defence against their Qurayshite adversaries.

THE SUITABILITY OF YATHRIB

The 'Aqaba pledges offered more than a friendly haven to the Muslims – Yathrib was uniquely fitted to become the base of the first Muslim community-state. Firstly, lying some 425 kilometres north of Makka, it was beyond any surprise punitive attack from the Quraysh, and, surrounded by mountains on almost three sides, was easily defensible. Secondly, in contrast to Makka, Taif, Yemen and Abyssinia, Yathrib did not enjoy a well-recognised, established political authority. Although 'Abdullah ibn Ubayy aspired to be crowned king, the Aws and the Khazraj, the two major tribes of Yathrib, were too divided to agree upon anyone as sovereign. And the Jews, though wealthy and influential, were not strong enough to control the state. Regarded as a foreign element, they had to enter into military pacts with various Arabian tribes to ensure their security. This should in no way be taken to mean that they were politically weak or unable to defend themselves; only that they may have felt themselves somewhat hemmed in by the warlike tribes of Yathrib and the surrounding regions. The recent war of Bu'āth between Aws and Khazraj had left behind it dark clouds of fear and insecurity. It was only natural that in such an environment people would look to their defences.

Thus, in Yathrib, there was a political vacuum, and the Yathribites did very well to invite the Prophet, upon him be peace, to move in, with the force of destiny, to fill it. They did not invite him merely as a temporary arbitrator in their time of difficulty but granted him full political authority, at the same time guaranteeing that authority with their lives[2].

Thirdly, being a fertile oasis, Yathrib had sufficient re-

---

[2] See below, pp. 98-9.

sources to provide not only for its inhabitants, but also for the influx of Muslim immigrants from Makka. There were enough palm trees and agricultural land to support a fast-growing community. The territory proved sufficient to withstand long military siege and the strains of a war economy – a vital factor for the nascent Muslim state during the many years of conflict with Makka, and hostility with the Bedouin tribes.

Fourthly, the Yathribites themselves were a great asset. The Aws and Khazraj were pure Arab tribes that had migrated from Yemen. Warlike and powerful in spirit, they responded with vigorous, active enthusiasm to the moral idealism of an Islamic community. Possessing the traditional Arab virtues of warmth and hospitality, they were wholly equal to the enormous difficulties of playing host to the impoverished and homeless Muhajirs (emigrants) from Makka. Tenderness of heart and friendly warmth were prominent traits of Yemeni Arabs – the Prophet, upon him be peace, on more than one occasion, commended the Yemenis for those traits[3].

Fifthly, Yathrib was ideally placed for an economic and psychological war of attrition against Makka: it commanded the route of the Makkan caravans to Syria. This strategic advantage was put to maximum use by the Prophet of Islam.

Lastly, but not least, of all the possible places that the Muslims might have migrated to, Yathrib alone enjoyed a direct association with all that was distinctly Arabian. It is this that Abyssinia and Egypt totally lacked, and Yemen and Syria possessed only in a very small measure. To have this Arabian association, the Muslim base had to be in the midst of the events in the Arabian peninsula – Makka and Taif were, of course, ruled out because of their hostility towards the Prophet, upon him be peace, and his call to Islam. In addition to being an Arab city, Yathrib had the further merit of being closer to the great urban centres of the so-called 'civilised' world – the Roman and Persian empires.

---

[3] The Prophet, upon him be peace, is reported to have praised the Yemeni very highly and thought very well of them. He is reported to have said: 'Here come the people of Yemen, tender of heart and good of intention. The *Īmān* (faith) is Yemeni and the *Hikmah* (wisdom) is Yemeni.' The Yemenis formed the strong core of the conquering Muslim forces that burst from the Arabian peninsula in the seventh century, seeking to spread the light of Islam in the whole universe.

2

The Muslim Exodus

HARDSHIPS AND SACRIFICES

Because the Muslim movement needed a base and because he could not prevent the Quraysh from persecuting his Companions – especially those who had no ties with the powerful clans of the Quraysh – the Prophet, upon him be peace, ordered the migration to Yathrib. The terms concluded in the second pledge with the Aws and Khazraj, were disclosed to the Muslims and the great exodus from Makka began. They received the order with mixed feelings of great relief and apprehension: the Hijra held out to them the promise of, at last, living freely and unmolested in accordance with the precepts of God and of the Qur'ān, but to give up home where they had lived for generations was no easy sacrifice to make. However it was the ideal that triumphed and drew from them the courage necessary to leave behind their homes, property and wealth. Ibn Hishām gives the names and the stories of these first heroes of Islam. Among the most moving is the story of Abū Salamah al-Makhzūmī and of his wife and their little child.

THE STORY OF ABŪ SALAMAH

According to Ibn Ḥishām, Abū Salamah al-Makhzūmī, a member of the prominent Qurayshite clan of Makhzūm (to which Khālid ibn Walīd also belonged) was the very first Muslim to migrate to Yathrib. Though protected by Abū Ṭālib, he suffered much maltreatment at the hands of the polytheists among the Quraysh. Naturally, after the death of Abū Ṭālib, Abū Salamah's sufferings intensified. As soon as he learned of the many conversions to Islam that had taken place in Yathrib – that is, even before the conclusion of the second 'Aqaba pledge – he put his wife and child on the back of a camel and, leading the animal himself, set off for Yathrib. Alas, he was observed by other unbelieving members of his family, relatives of his wife, who said, 'If we can do nothing about you, surely you can't take away our woman', and prevented his wife, Umm Salamah, from going with him. When the relatives of Abū Salamah heard of this, they vowed not to leave the little child (Salamah) with his maternal uncles, so they came and took the boy away from his mother. Thus Umm Salamah, deprived of both husband and son, was left behind alone. Her estrangement from her unbelieving family worsened the anguish of her predicament. The separation from both her immediate family and her social environment was total, and she had to endure the afflictions of heart and mind in utter isolation. Each day she would walk out of the family's quarters and sit in some high place, fixing her eyes aimlessly upon the horizon. She would then weep and weep till the sun went down, when she would turn back and walk slowly home. This continued for a whole year until a relative, walking by, was moved to compassion for her. He went to her clan and entreated on her behalf, saying how she was wronged in this enforced separation from husband and son. At length, her clan agreed that she should be allowed to join her husband in Yathrib. Then her son was returned to her and she set out immediately – but without provisions[1] and all alone – in the direction of Yathrib. She and her son, Salamah, rode on a solitary she-camel. After she had gone some distance, 'Uthmān Ṭalḥah, an idolator from the Quraysh, came by and, on realising that she was going alone to Yathrib, offered to act as her guide and protector. She accepted, and he escorted her all the way to Yathrib, taking great care not to invade her privacy, nor take advantage of her in any way. When they dismounted to rest, he would retreat to a distant tree. His courtesy and nobility greatly impressed Umm Salamah. When, at the edge of Yathrib, the houses of Qubā' came into sight, he bade her goodbye and started back towards Makka. In later times, Umm Salamah would remember that 'No one has suffered more than the House of Abū Salamah', and recall

[1] She thought she would be able to get food from travellers along the road.

that she could not have found a journey companion nobler than 'Uthmān ibn Ṭalḥah.

THE JAḤSH FAMILY

After Abū Salamah, among these first immigrants to Madina were 'Āmir ibn Rabī'ah, an ally of Banū 'Adī ibn Ka'b, accompanied by his wife, Layla, daughter of Ḥathmah. Also, and as we shall see, more significantly, all the household of 'Abdullah ibn Jaḥsh, including 'Abdullah ibn Jaḥsh himself and his immediate family and his brother Abd, better known as Abū Aḥmad. Abū Aḥmad was a blind poet who used to go unguided everywhere in Makka. He was married to al Fāri'ah bint Abū Sufyān, and his mother, 'Umaymah, was daughter of 'Abd al-Muṭṭalib (aunt of the Prophet).

As the whole family migrated, their house was locked up. A group of Qurayshite leaders passing by on one occasion, saw the house of 'Abdullah ibn Jaḥsh, empty and deserted, its doors rocking in the wind. They were deeply moved and one of them, 'Utbah ibn Rabī'ah, father of Hind bint 'Utbah (Abū Sufyān's wife, who was nicknamed 'the chewer of livers' because she chewed the liver of Ḥamzah, after the Battle of Uḥud), sighed heavily and then recited some verses of Arabic poetry. The sense of these verses is: 'Every house, no matter how long it has endured in peace will one day be caught up in tragedy and suffering'. This indicates that the family of 'Abdullah ibn Jaḥsh was noted for its prosperity and that happiness and security were conspicuous features of their life in Makka. This is hardly surprising if we consider the powerful links that this family had with the two leading clans of Quraysh, namely Hāshimites and Makhzūmites. These two clans were the chief strength of the Makkan Qurayshite aristocracy. Yet, Islam had irrecoverably changed the Jaḥshs' life and outlook. To go on living in Makka, in that happy and familiar house, was no longer feasible. Islam had changed their aspiration for ever, as it had done with all those early Muslims. Abū Jahl, who was with 'Utbah, bitterly blamed the Prophet Muhammad, upon him be peace, for the departure of the Jaḥsh family. The whole of Makka seems to have missed them, a fact that encouraged Abū Jahl to press the usual charges against the Prophet of having divided the community and disturbed its peace.

There can be no doubt that the migration of the Jaḥsh family, so much at the centre of the city's social life, persuaded and inspired other Muslims to follow their example. There were, first of all, the many relatives of 'Abdullah ibn Jaḥsh who would have missed him and his poet brother, Abū Aḥmad – among these were the beautiful and charming Zaynab, daughter of Jaḥsh, later married to the Prophet, and Umm Ḥabībah and Ḥamnah, also Jaḥsh's daughters. Other prominent early immigrants to Yathrib included 'Ukkāshah ibn Miḥṣin and 'Amr ibn Miḥṣin, 'Ukkāshah brothers; the brothers Shujā' ibn Wahb and 'Uqbah ibn Wahb; Arbad ibn Ḥumayyirah; Munqidh ibn Nubātah; the brothers Sa'īd and Yazīd ibn Ruqaysh; Muḥriz ibn Naḍlah; Qays ibn Jābir; the brothers Mālik, Ṣafwān and Thaqf ibn 'Amr; Rabī'ah ibn Aktham; and the brothers Al-Zubayr ibn 'Ubayd, Tammām ibn 'Ubaydah and Sakhbarah ibn 'Ubaydah. The first five in this list were related to the House of Jaḥsh – a fact that further confirms their influence in Makka – the common ancestor being, it seems, Ghanm ibn Dūdān.

The poet Abū Aḥmad must, through his poetry, have played a particularly significant part in motivating others to make the Hijra. In moving verse he called for the Hijra, honouring those who forsook the warmth and familiar comforts of home and friends, seeking instead a place where they might live according to their convictions, in peace and dignity. He payed tribute to his clan of Ghanm ibn Dūdān of Banū Asad ibn Khuzaymah, recalling that they, Banū Ghanm ibn Dūdān, were distinguished and ancient dwellers of Makka. Their descendants were still men of prominence and great standing – if they decided to migrate it was not on account of rootlessness or any lack in lineage or social prestige. Rather, it was because they wished to fulfil religious aspirations and gain favour in the eyes of God and of His messenger, Muhammad, upon him be peace. Referring to an altercation he had with his wife (Umm Aḥmad) on the morning that he was preparing to begin his Hijra, he reiterated the religious motives that inspired him. The same motives, he argued against his wife, justified the destination of the Hijra – Yathrib, an Arabian city. His wife's hesitation is understandable, however: to a Makkan the relatively humid air of Yathrib was detestable and, indeed, many citizens of Yathrib were, at this time, affected by malaria.

While expressing his heart's sadness at the compelled parting from sincere friends and from the women who wept bitterly in their grief, Abū Aḥmad also strongly denied the allegation – doubtless expressed by some critics of their projected departure – that they were seeking to avenge their persecution at the hands of the Quraysh. He affirmed that, on the contrary, he was setting out only in the hope of the good things to come – the ideals he hoped to realise, and the freedom from persecution so badly lacking in Makka. Finally, he urged his clansmen to be steadfast in their religious conviction even though some of their Quraysh cousins were hostile and indeed aided others in persecuting and tormenting them – thus, by implication, Abū Aḥmad invited them to undertake the Hijra. He expressed the familiar truth that men ever divide into two distinct factions – those who accept and those who oppose the truth. His clansmen would do well not to grieve over Quraysh unbelief and insolence.

Abū Sufyān sells the house of Jaḥsh. Ibn Hishām names, besides the Jaḥsh, only two families all of whose members made the Hijra – Makhzūm and al-Bukayr. The houses of these families were locked up for lack of tenants and then left deserted. As if to punish the family of Jaḥsh for their departure, Abū Sufyān usurped their empty house and sold it. The positive significance of the Hijra was not lost upon the Quraysh and their anger and frustration were, therefore, hardly surprising: they may even have felt threatened by the gathering of the Muslims in Yathrib.

Equally human was the reaction of 'Abdullah ibn Jaḥsh to the loss of his house. Deeply troubled by it, he spoke to the Prophet, upon him be peace, who, looking at him with great compassion, said:

> 'O 'Abdullah, are you not satisfied if God gives you a better house in Paradise?'
> 'Yes', replied 'Abdullah, well pleased by the offer.
> 'Then it is yours', replied the Prophet, upon him be peace.

Apparently 'Abdullah ibn Jaḥsh made no further mention of the subject. However, his brother, the poet Abū Aḥmad, quite naturally hoped to regain their house after Makka was victoriously captured by the Muslims. He expressed this view before the Prophet, who gave no answer, keeping silent; perhaps he even showed signs of displeasure, unnoticed by the blind Abū Aḥmad. But the people present at the time told Abū Aḥmad that the Prophet had not liked his query about his lost property. That property was lost in the fight in the way of God and ought not to be reclaimed in this world: he should not, the people advised him, raise the subject again with the Prophet. That advice was properly heeded by Abū Aḥmad; but he did compose a verse censuring Abū Sufyān for having usurped their house and sold it illegally.

THE HIJRA OF 'UMAR IBN AL-KHAṬṬĀB

Ibn Hishām's account of the emigration of 'Umar to Yathrib is remarkable for its omission of the popular story of 'Umar's openly declared emigration and his challenge to the Quraysh to try and stop him. But the omission is surely intelligent – it is much more credible that 'Umar made his exit from Makka under the cover of darkness. Nor was he alone – here too, Ibn Hishām is at variance with the popular version, to be found in Ibn Kathîr, in which he did set out alone and in broad daylight – but went in the company of 'Ayyāsh ibn Abū Rabî'ah al-Makhzūmî. This brought the number of well-known Makhzūmites who made the Hijra in this early period to three – the first two being Abū Salamah and 'Abdullah ibn Jaḥsh.

The Hijra of 'Ayyāsh involved an interesting episode, narrated by 'Umar ibn al-Khaṭṭāb himself. He says that he had made an appointment with two other Muslims, namely 'Ayyāsh and Hishām ibn al-'Āṣ al-Sahmî, to meet the following day in the early morning outside Makka. They also agreed not to wait if any of them failed to turn up at the appointed time, because they were anticipating that the Quraysh would try to impede them or, failing that, pursue them. 'Umar says that Hishām was detained and forced to recant his faith. 'Umar and 'Ayyāsh, however, managed to make their Hijra safely to Yathrib. But not for long, as Abū Jahl and his brother, al-Hārith, soon arrived in Yathrib. 'Ayyāsh was the son of their uncle who was previously married to their mother and so was their maternal brother. They might even have set out in pursuit of him, but if they did, they concealed it with great care. They contrived a story to the effect that their mother had vowed never to comb her hair, nor move from under the sun, until 'Ayyāsh came back, or until her death. When he heard the story, 'Ayyāsh was deeply moved on account of this alleged suffering of his mother. He was inclined to accompany Abū Jahl and al-Hārith back to Makka, saying that he would thus release his mother from her vow and that, besides, he had left his money behind and could perhaps bring some of it back. 'Umar says that he suspected the plot from the start, and did his best to talk 'Ayyāsh out of the idea of going – he even promised 'Ayyāsh half his own wealth if he did not go, and urged that 'Ayyāsh's mother would soon comb her hair if lice were to cause her any trouble, and if the heat of Makka oppressed her she would not hesitate to take shelter from it. But 'Ayyāsh was determined. 'Umar's suspicions were soon confirmed, for 'Ayyāsh was overpowered by his two maternal brothers and, with hands bound, taken to Makka. Here they tortured him and forced him to recant his faith.

There was widespread general sympathy among the Muslims for the two faithful Muslims detained in Makka and tortured by the Quraysh. For this reason, as soon as he had settled in Madina after his Hijra, the Prophet, upon him be peace, arranged for their rescue. It was first revealed that God had forgiven their weakness of recanting their faith under torture. The Qur'ānic verse on this occasion reads:

> Say: O my servants who have been prodigal against yourselves, do not despair of God's mercy; surely God forgives all sins; surely He is the Forgiving, the Merciful. (al-Zumar, 39: 53)

Al-Walīd ibn al-Walīd ibn al-Mughīrah, the Muslim son of the infamous al-Walīd ibn Mughīrah, paramount chief of Makhzūm and father of Khālid ibn al-Walīd, volunteered to carry out the daring commando operation of rescuing the two detained Muslims. The captives as well as their captors were members of his own clan of Makhzūm. Al-Walīd ibn al-Walīd ibn al-Mughīrah made his way secretly to Makka. He was fortunate enough to discover the woman employed to feed the

Muslim prisoners. By following her unnoticed, he located the room where they were being held. It was roofless, so he waited for the cover of darkness and climbed in over the wall. With his sword, he cut the captives' chains against a stone and the three of them got away to Madina. They were received with great joy and al-Walīd was greatly admired.The sword with which he cut the chains against the stone was thenceforth greatly cherished, and given the honorific title, Dhu al-Marwah – 'the sword that cut into the stone.'

ZAYNAB, DAUGHTER OF MUHAMMAD

The separation of Zaynab, daughter of the Prophet Muhammad from his marriage to Khadījah, and her subsequent emigration to Madina, is one of the most moving dramas of the Muslim exodus. According to Islam, a Muslim woman cannot be joined in marriage to a non-Muslim man. But Ibn Ḥishām records that such mixed families continued to exist during the Makkan period. He ascribes this phenomenon to the Prophet's lack of political authority, his condition being described as circumscribed. He was, in particular, unable to separate women who had become Muslims from their unbelieving husbands. So Zaynab continued to live with her husband, Abū al-'Āṣ ibn al-Rabī', to whom she was bound with the strongest bonds of love and affection. Abū al-'Āṣ ibn al-Rabī' was, according to Ibn Hishām, among the few most distinguished Makkans: he belonged to the clan of 'Abd Shams, on his father's side, and the clan of Banū Asad, on his mother's, and had (by pre-Islamic standards) enjoyed noble birth and upbringing. He was also blessed with almost every other advantage that could be hoped for – handsome looks, wealth and very fine manners. His mother had, apparently, died whilst he was young, and her cousin, Khadījah, felt a very special affection for him, and had him brought up in her own house. Such was her fondness that, according to Ibn Hishām, she considered him as her own. It was a death-bed wish of hers that he should marry one of her daughters. That wish was fulfilled, quite naturally, as Abū al-'Āṣ developed a great love for Zaynab. Zaynab (like her mother Khadījaḥ) was blessed with a warm character, sound independent judgement, and boundless affection and tenderness. Zaynab's marriage to Abū al-'Āṣ took place before the commencement of Muhammad's prophethood, upon him be peace. His second daughter from Khadījah, Umm Kulthūm, was married to her cousin 'Utbah, son of the infamous Abū Lahab, the Prophet's unbelieving uncle. When, later, the Quraysh were anxious to do what hurt they could to the Prophet, they tried to persuade Abū al-'Āṣ and 'Utbah to divorce their wives, the Prophet's daughters. 'Utbah complied, but Abū al-'Āṣ adamantly refused to divorce Zaynab. Naturally, the Prophet was very moved and impressed by this manly independence of spirit, and his affection for his son-in-law must have increased. When Abū al-'Āṣ fell captive in the Battle of Badr, it was an opportunity to show well-deserved clemency towards him. The Prophet set him free without accepting his ransom, which incidentally was to be paid by Zaynab herself, who was still in Makka at the time. The ransom was none other than the well-known object of Khadījah's favourite wedding ring. Another occasion on which Abū al-'Āṣ was favourably treated was when his caravan was raided by the Muslims in the vicinity of Madina shortly before the final conquest of Makka. He managed to escape, though the caravan was taken by the Muslims, and, under cover of night, made his way to the house of Zaynab who was now living with her father in Madina, separated from her husband because of religion. He asked for her protection and she gave it. The Prophet later endorsed and honoured her action, but instructed her to keep at a distance from him, matrimonial intimacy being forbidden, as he was still an unbeliever. But Abū al-'Āṣ stayed in the house of the Prophet.

Zaynab sets out for Madina. The manner in which Abū al-'Āṣ had let Zaynab go from Makka, at the Prophet's request, and migrate to Madina provides a further indication of the nobility of his character. Still an unbeliever, and an active participant in the hostilities that the Quraysh were conducting against Islam, he never hesitated to honour the Prophet's wish that he be separated from Zaynab. Nevertheless, Zaynab's journey to Madina was not without tragedy. Ibn Hishām tells the story thus:

The journey took place roughly a month after Badr. The

Prophet sent his adopted son, Zayd ibn Hārithah, and one of the Ansar to go out to fetch her. They stayed in Yā'jaj, some eight miles north of Makka. Meanwhile, Zaynab was preparing for the journey in absolute secrecy; being the Prophet's daughter, she knew the value of secrecy when a major task is being undertaken. Of course, the Quraysh were watching, and it is most improbable that they would willingly have granted the Prophet the satisfaction and blessing of being reunited with his daughter, especially when this reunion had a religious significance for him. So Zaynab had to plan her exit from Makka very carefully. In particular, she had to dodge the watchful eyes of the vengeful Hind bint 'Utbah ibn Rabī'ah, wife of Abū Sufyān:

> 'O daughter of Muhammad. Did I hear that you are going off to rejoin your father?'
>
> 'No, I have no such wish.'
>
> 'O daughter of my uncle, do not go. Yet, if you must, allow me to provide such things as you may need on the journey – money too. You have only to tell me – please do not be shy of me. Whatever misunderstanding exists between men should not be allowed to undermine the friendship between women.'

Zaynab thought that Hind was sincere in her offers but reaffirmed her denial of any intended journey, and went on with her secret preparations. When everything was ready, her brother-in-law, Kinānah ibn al-Rabī', decided it was safe to leave with her in broad daylight: he may have thought that as she was inside a Hawdaj (Howdah) nobody would notice that it was she. If so, he was proven wholly wrong. Soon, Quraysh horsemen were in hot pursuit. They caught up with Zaynab and her guide in a place not far from Makka called Dhāt al-Ṭawa. One of the pursuers, called Habbār ibn al-Aswad, threatened her with his spear. The camel too must have been frightened by this, for it jerked violently and Zaynab, who was pregnant, fell so heavily to the ground that her unborn child was killed. In this way, Zaynab's skilful handling of Hind, all her patient, secret preparations, were rendered futile by the reckless and thoughtless action of her well-meaning brother-in-law, Kinānah. He did, however, manage to push back the offenders and guard Zaynab against any further injury. At length, a deputation of Qurayshite elders arrived on the scene. They upbraided Kinānah for the way he had made his exit from the city. He had been insensitive they argued, to the feelings of the Quraysh against Muhammad, especially after the heavy casualties they had suffered in the recent Battle of Badr. If they had allowed him to take her in broad daylight, this would have been interpreted by the Arab tribes as a sign of weakness or even cowardice on the part of the Quraysh. Then, Abū Sufyān, acting as the paramount chief of the Quraysh (which he no doubt was after the death of Abū Jahl and other Quraysh leaders at Badr) assured Zaynab and her brother-in-law that they would, after all, be allowed to make their journey to Madina, but must leave at night and in secrecy. After a few days, when things were more calm and settled, Zaynab was allowed to make the journey as promised. She safely made her way to Madina and was reunited with her father, the Prophet, upon him be peace.

Repercussions of the Zaynab episode. When news of the maltreatment of Zaynab reached Madina, the Prophet and the Muslims were horrified and enraged: such an act against a woman is repugnant to the Muslim as well as to the Arab mind. The Prophet's reaction was, naturally, compounded by his personal involvement. He dispatched a military squad, ordering them to seize the two offenders, especially Habbār, and burn them to death. Later, however, he relented and ordered their execution by the sword, should the offenders be apprehended. The sympathy for Zaynab was widespread. Many poets, Muslim as well as non-Muslim, expressed their disapproval and horror at the incident. Even Hind bint 'Utbah ibn Rabī'ah, wife of Abū Sufyān, is reported to have composed a verse condemning the attackers of Zaynab and describing them as cowards, who had failed to prove their courage on the battlefield at Badr. If this report is correct, then Hind was indeed sincere in her offers to help Zaynab move to Madina.

Ultimately, the whole affair did much to discredit the Quraysh in the eyes of the Arabs, who consider aggression against women as utter cowardice, absolutely repugnant to their sense of chivalry. However, the favourable view of Zaynab's husband, Abū al-'Āṣ, and his family, was further improved in the eyes of the Muslims when Abū al-'Āṣ fell into Muslim hands for the second time, just before the conquest of Makka: Zaynab extended her protection to him, without even asking the Prophet's permission. Nobody objected to her move, nor even questioned it. It was accepted with an understanding and sympathy, richly deserved. Shortly afterwards, Abū al-'Āṣ himself embraced Islam, and was reunited with his wife after many years of separation and agony. This brought to an end one of the most moving dramas of early Islamic history.

THE MEANING OF SACRIFICE: ṢUHAYB THE ROMAN

These stories of the Muslim exodus doubtless represent only a very partial record of many examples of heroism, suffering and endurance. But that the early Muslims were, in a sense, heroes, men and women of extraordinary spirit and vision, there can be no doubt. The Hijra itself emerges as one of the most striking instances of the invincibility of human aspirations towards the highest ideals of truth, goodness and liberty. As God is the grantor and embodiment of these ideals, the Hijra was therefore not merely a flight from darkness and tyranny but an active seeking of Him. The full significance of Hijra will become clearer in the account of the Prophet's own Hijra. However we conclude the present chapter with the story of Ṣuhayb al-Rūmī, Ṣuhayb the Roman. Learning of his intended flight, the Quraysh approached him and said: 'You came to us poor and dispossessed. Now that you have amassed great wealth from amongst us, do you think we will let you move away with it?' Ṣuhayb hesitated not at all – 'Take it,' said he, 'take it all. Only let me go.' When the Prophet, upon him be peace, heard how Ṣuhayb had sacrificed all his wealth, he commented – 'Ṣuhayb has won. Indeed Ṣuhayb has won.'

3

The Hijra of the Prophet and Abū Bakr

After his return from his unfruitful journey to Taif, the Prophet, upon him be peace, strongly felt that Makka was not, and could not become, his abode. Its polytheists had rejected the message of truth, refused to heed the Divine Call to worship the One, True God. This rejection only further confirmed that those people of Makka were determined upon evil ways, and it doomed them irrevocably. Their social structures would have to be destroyed, by force if necessary. The violence with which the Makkans had treated the Prophet and his Companions made armed resistance not only justifiable, but – especially after the deaths of Abū Ṭālib and Khadījah – imperative and urgent. Abū Bakr, more than anyone else, shared the Prophet's uneasiness, as well as his aspirations to a more sympathetic social environment. The gradual diminution of the city's Muslim population must have intensified the feelings of loneliness and alienation growing in the sensitive soul of Abū Bakr: 'Will you give me permission to migrate, O Prophet of God?' he would ask. And back would come the Prophet's assurance: 'Don't be in a hurry; it may be that God will give you a companion.' Abū Bakr wished, deep in his heart, that this promised companion would be the Prophet himself. At that time no Muslims were left in Makka, except for the Prophet, upon him be peace, Abū Bakr and 'Ali ibn Abū Ṭālib, and those who were confined by the Quraysh or forced to recant their faith.

THE QURAYSH ASSEMBLE AND PLOT TO KILL THE PROPHET

So disturbed were the Quraysh by the gathering of the Muslims in Yathrib that they called an urgent meeting at Dār al-Nadwah, their assembly place. Formerly, it had been the house of Quṣayy ibn Kilāb, great-grandfather of the Prophet, upon him be peace. In that meeting, they decided that the best way to get rid of the Prophet for ever was to assassinate him. To avoid a blood feud with the Hāshimites and their allies the Muṭṭalibites, they decided that the clans would be represented in a special murder squad, formed especially for this unholy mission. But God revealed the whole affair to the Prophet through the Angel Gabriel. The long-awaited hour of undertaking the Hijra had come. According to Ibn Hishām, the Prophet then came out through the main gate of his house. As he went past the idolators, he recited the following Qur'ānic verses and, says Ibn Hishām, scattered dust over their heads, passing by them as if invisible:[1]

> '*Yā, Sīn.*
> By the Wise Qur'ān,
> Surely, you are of the Apostles
> on a straight path.
> A revelation from the Mighty, the Merciful,
> That you may warn a people
> whose fathers were never warned
> So they are heedless.
> The word has been proved against most of them,
> yet they do not believe.
> Surely We have put on their necks fetters,
> up to the chin, so their heads are raised.
> And We have put before them a barrier,
> and behind them a barrier,
> and We have blurred their sight, so that they do not see.' (Yā Sīn, 36: 1-9)

These Qur'ānic verses, believed to have had a mysterious effect upon the plotters, preventing them from seeing the Prophet, are recited by pious Muslims even today on similar occasions of great peril. They are thought to shield the righteous Muslims from their enemies.

In the early morning, the plotters discovered that the

---

[1] Ibn Sa'd's version is substantially similar to Ibn Hishām. The only significant difference is that Ibn Sa'd says that the Prophet spent the whole day hiding in Abū Bakr's house, and only ventured outside under cover of night. Ibn Sa'd, Vol. 1.

Prophet had slipped away during the night. According to al-Suhaylī, the plotters were prevented from breaking into the house at night by the cries of a woman inside. They were wary in case the neighbours should come to know of their break-in. This would have led to their censure by the Arabs, who did not sanction such actions, especially where a woman was involved. The only hope for the Quraysh now was to catch the Prophet before he reached his destination.

THE PROPHET IN ABŪ BAKR'S HOUSE

After leaving his house, the Prophet did not go directly to the house of Abū Bakr – he arrived there at midday, and our sources do not specify where he spent the morning. Quite possibly, he hid in the house of one of his relatives from among the Hāshimites. At any rate, around midday he entered the house of Abū Bakr, an unexpected visitor at the hottest hour of the day. 'Ā'ishah, daughter of Abū Bakr, said the Prophet, upon him be peace, was used to visiting them every day, either in the morning or the evening, but never at noon. When Abū Bakr saw him come in at that unusual hour, he said: 'Whatever has brought the Prophet out at this hour of the day must be a very important matter.' When the Prophet, upon him be peace, entered, Abū Bakr stood up and offered his seat, which reverence and hospitality the Prophet accepted, but then asked of Abū Bakr that he send those present out of the room. 'But they are only my daughters,' replied Abū Bakr, 'and they can do no harm; may my father and mother be your ransom!' The Prophet explained that God had given him permission to migrate to Yathrib. 'Together, O Messenger of God?' anxiously asked Abū Bakr. 'Together,' replied the Prophet. Abū Bakr's eyes were filled with tears. 'Ā'ishah recalled that she had never before thought that people could cry because of joy, until she saw her noble father weep at the prospect of accompanying the Prophet, whom he loved so dearly, to Yathrib. Then Abū Bakr said that he had hoped for this all along, since the Prophet had told him that God might give him a companion. He also informed the Prophet of the two camels which he had long since purchased, in anticipation of the journey. The two camels were very well looked after by Abū Bakr. Abū Bakr had also already arranged the hiring of a very good guide to take them on the road to Yathrib – the man was a polytheist, not a Muslim, but expert and completely trustworthy. His name was 'Abdullah ibn Arqaṭ. The Prophet insisted on paying the cost of his camel, thus indicating the importance and desirability of each Muslim paying, as far as possible, the expenses of his own Hijra.

PLANNING THE HIJRA

The Prophet, upon him be peace, planned both his exit from Makka, and the route he would take to Yathrib, most carefully. Very likely he did not stay long in the house of Abū Bakr:[2] perhaps one or two hours, enough time for Abū Bakr to make the necessary contacts and arrangements for the journey – their guide would have to be instructed and food and other provisions got ready.

When preparations were complete, possibly by mid afternoon, the Prophet, upon him be peace, and Abū Bakr slipped out, using a little window at the back of the house, which opens in the direction of the hills. They avoided the main streets of the city, walking rather than riding, so as not to be noticed. To mislead their pursuers even further, they went southwards, that is, in a direction opposite the one normally taken for Yathrib. The Prophet knew quite well that his pursuers would be waiting for him on the Yathrib road to the north of Makka. His immediate destination was a cave in the Mount of Thawr, just below the city of Makka to the south. Things were well planned in advance, so that they could hide safely for three days in that cave, a period sufficient for things to calm down, and to draw the pursuers off the road.

'Abdullah ibn Abū Bakr was to be an intelligence agent, he was to listen to the talk of the city, and to the consultation of the Quraysh during the day, and bring back news of the day's events at night. Asmā', daughter of Abū Bakr, was to bring some food at night. Abū Bakr's freed-man, 'Āmir ibn Fuhayrah, was instructed to drive his flock to the cave by night. In this way, they would have fresh milk and fresh meat

[2] Ibn Sa'd's version, which we indicated before, stipulates that the Prophet spent the whole day in Abū Bakr's house – an unlikely scheme, given the circumstances of the hot pursuit by the Quraysh. Even if the Prophet decided to hide in Makka for the rest of that day, Abū Bakr's house would not have been the ideal place.

every evening. Also, the sheep's tracks would cover the tracks of 'Abdullah ibn Abū Bakr, as he shuttled between the cave and Makka.

After three days in the cave, when the Prophet and Abū Bakr were ready to be on the road again, Asmā' came along with a big bag of provisions for the journey. She wanted to fasten it to one of the camels, but she could not find a string to tie it with. She improvised by tearing her own girdle in half and made a string from it. For this reason, this noble and courageous young woman who, later, was married to the celebrated Companion of the Prophet, al-Zubayr ibn al-'Awwām, was called 'she of the two girdles'.

THE MIRACLE OF THE CAVE

The miracle of the cave is omitted by Ibn Hishām, but Ibn Sa'd mentions it[3] and some accounts in Hadith confirm that it occurred. Aḥmad ibn Ḥanbal, in his *Musnad,* narrated that 'the polytheists followed the track of the Prophet and his Companion until they reached the Mount of Thawr; when they could no longer follow the track some of them climbed the mount until they came to the cave in which the Prophet and Abū Bakr were hiding. But they were discouraged from entering by the cobwebs covering the entrance of the cave. They said one to another: Had he entered the cave, the cobwebs would not have been undisturbed.'[4]

It is significant that the version of the *Musnad* does not mention either a tree whose branches hung over the entrance or wild pigeons that had made their nests and laid their eggs in the opening of the cave, which are found in some accounts. However, both Bukhārī and Muslim mention that the Quraysh pursuers actually came to the cave, though they did not allude to the miracle of the cobweb, the tree or the pigeons. Abū Bakr worried so much about the safety of the Prophet, upon him be peace, that he shook with fear. But the Prophet

---

[3] Ibn Sa'd's *Al-Tabaqāt al-Kubrā*, Vol. 1, pp. 228, 229 ff. (Bayrout, Dar Sādir). Ibn Sa'd's version mentions the cobwebs, the tree and the two wild pigeons.

[4] *Al Musnad* of Ibn Ḥanbal. The miracle of the cave is also mentioned by Ibn Kathīr (*al-Bidāyah*) and by al Ḥāfiz (*al-Fatḥ*). However, some authorities of Hadith regard it as weakly supported.

reassured him: 'Oh Abū Bakr, what do you think of two men whose third is God Himself.' The Qur'ān itself alludes to the exchange between the Prophet and Abū Bakr. When the polytheists were standing above the cave, Abū Bakr said: 'If one of them were to look beneath his feet, he would see us, O Prophet of God.' And the Prophet answered him: 'Do not grieve. God is surely with us.'

Alluding to the above dialogue, the following Qur'ānic verses were revealed:

> ... If you do not help him yet God has helped him already. When those who disbelieve drove him forth, the second of the two, when they were in the cave, when he said to his companion, 'Grieve not, surely God is with us' then God sent down upon him His peace and security (*Sakīna*) and supported him with legions you did not see.
>
> And He made the word of those who disbelieved the lowest and the word of God the uppermost, God is Almighty, All Wise. (al-Tawbah, 9: 40)

Understandably, the prize of one hundred camels which the Quraysh had offered to anyone who captured the Prophet and Abū Bakr, was so tempting that young men were in pursuit on every possible track. Thus a band of them climbed Mount Thawr, up to the hiding place. Yet, strangely, though they came to the opening of the cave, they did not enter, nor even look inside. The miracle of the cave, though not mentioned in the Qur'ān or Bukhārī and Muslim, nor even Ibn Hishām, plays an explanatory role, without which the failure of the pursuers is inexplicable.

After the third night in the cave of Mount Thawr, 'Abdullah ibn Arqaṭ brought the camels, two for the Prophet and Abū Bakr and a third for himself. The Prophet, upon him be peace, mounted first and insisted on buying the camel from Abū Bakr; Abū Bakr and his freed-man 'Āmir ibn Fuhayrah, rode on the second camel. The three lonely riders thus began their long and perilous journey to Yathrib. They avoided the usual route as much as possible and their expert guide was exceptionally useful in this respect. They had to ride fast for almost all the night and most of the day. They could not afford to go slowly because they knew very well what unthinkable horrors awaited them should the Quraysh succeed in catching them.

THE ROUTE OF THE PROPHET'S HIJRA

From Makka, they first headed for the shore of the Red Sea. They went parallel to the sea until they reached a place called 'Usfān. From here they turned a little inland and travelled for some distance along the foot of Mount Amaj. Then they followed a route parallel to the usual route, carefully avoiding the latter. They went past Qudayda, al-Kharrār, Thanniyya al-Marrah and Liqfā (all of them small places on the route to Yathrib), and crossed the territory of the tribe of Madlijah. Beyond that, they made rest stops at several places. They crossed the territories of the tribes of Aslam, where the Prophet, upon him be peace, hired a camel to relieve his own which was exhausted by the long non-stop journey. Before they entered Qubā', they passed through such places as al-'Araj, Thanniyya al-Ghā'ir and the valley of Ri'm. But a mere list of place names cannot convey the drama and meaning of the journey. News of the Prophet's Hijra spread across the desert with the swiftness of fire, and the whole of Arabia was involved. But, of course, the most intense stir was in Makka and Yathrib – the news was received with desperate anger and frustration or, at the other extreme, on a rising tide of love and expectation.

AT ABŪ BAKR'S HOUSE : TWO VISITORS

At the house of Abū Bakr, there was a great feeling of rejoicing and excitement, and a certain air of accomplishment, even of adventure. The two remarkable daughters of Abū Bakr and his son, 'Abdullah, rejoiced greatly, delighted to have played their part in helping the Prophet and Abū Bakr, the two men they loved more than anything else, to get away from Makka. First, it was Abū Jahl and other Quraysh leaders who called. Asmā' opened the door. 'Where is your father?' demanded Abū Jahl. 'I do not know,' answered Asmā'. Then, she said, Abū Jahl slapped her face until one of her face ornaments was sent flying in the air.

Second to call was Abū Quḥāfah, Abū Bakr's father, an old, blind man who was worried, among other things, about how he would support his son's family now that he had gone. He asked whether Abū Bakr had left any money. Knowing that the old man would be quite upset if he was told the truth (Abū Bakr had taken all his money), Asmā' had to devise a trick to calm and reassure the old man, even if this meant some untruthfulness on her part. 'Would you put your hand into this,' she said, guiding his hand into a bag containing stones. 'You see,' she went on, 'father has left us enough money'. The trick worked and the old man was duly reassured.

Both incidents tell a great deal about the promise of this young girl of Abū Bakr's and say something too about Abū Bakr himself in the way that he brought her up. Asmā' was later married to al-Zubayr ibn al-'Awwām, and her son was the famous 'Abdullah ibn al-Zubayr.

THE SURĀQAH INCIDENT

The Prophet's party could not have gone very far, when there appeared on the horizon a horseman, galloping full speed towards them. According to Ibn Hishām, the Prophet was still within the territory of the tribe of Madlijah. He could not have gone very far from Makka. Possibly the incident took place on the second day after the Prophet left the cave. According to Ibn Hishām's account, Surāqah learned of the whereabouts of the Prophet from a traveller, a stranger, who came to Makka from Banū Mudlaj. Anxious to get the prize of a hundred camels, he gulled the traveller into keeping the matter quiet after he had casually mentioned the riders on the road. He hinted darkly to the stranger about the identity of the riders, naming them as Banū So-and-So. Then he stole out of Makka in pursuit. Before he set out, he drew lots which were unfavourable, but decided to go on just the same. When he was in sight of the Prophet, his horse fell twice. But he persisted in the chase. As he drew still nearer, his horse fell so badly that its forehooves sank deep in the sand. The animal managed to pull its hooves out, and there followed a column of smoke. Surāqah was very frightened and it became impressed on his mind that the Prophet, upon him be peace, and his party were protected from him by Divine force. He called out loudly, naming himself and vowing that he intended no harm. The Prophet and his Companions waited for him.

When he had come up to them, Abū Bakr, at the Prophet's suggestion, asked him what he wanted. 'Only a document from you,' Surāqah replied, 'a document that will be an evidence between you and me'. Presumably, Surāqah wanted the document as proof of the strange encounter – possibly he hoped that he might get some credit for it in years to come. Abū Bakr wrote him the paper and Surāqah bade them good-bye and departed in peace, pledging that he would not disclose their whereabouts to the Quraysh, a pledge which he kept.

The incident must have occurred while the Prophet and Abū Bakr were travelling along the common road, otherwise it would have been very difficult for Surāqah to find them.

OTHER INCIDENTS ON THE WAY

Other incidents, less dramatic than that of Surāqah but nevertheless interesting, include a refreshing meal, after the Prophet's first night on the road, provided by a generous Bedouin widow in the encampment of the Khuzā'ah, a tribe that lived in the vicinity of Makka, and was later caught in the struggle between the Prophet and the Quraysh. The widow was called Umm Ma'bad, daughter of Ka'b. After spending all of the first night on the road, the Prophet and his party descended on her hungry and exhausted in the early hours of the day. They asked to buy food from her, but she hadn't much to offer. In the end, she gave them cool, fresh goat's milk, which they drank until completely satisfied. The Prophet's visit to the tent of Umm Ma'bad, in the encampment of Khuzā'ah, happened before the Surāqah incident.

It is also reported that the Prophet and Abū Bakr met with Ṭalḥah, Abū Bakr's son-in-law, and his cousin. Ṭalḥah was returning from Syria with his caravan. He had passed through Yathrib and was able to supply comforting news from there. The city was waiting impatiently for the arrival of the Prophet and news that he had quit Makka had spread far and wide. Ṭalḥah's report must have been extremely heartening after the tension and danger they had just come through. It was also reported that he gave new garments as gifts to both the Prophet and Abū Bakr. These must have been most welcome after five or more days on the road with little opportunity to change clothes. The Prophet and his companion must have felt a great sense of relief and security. They were no longer fugitives in danger of being caught by their enemy; rather, they were all but out of reach of the Quraysh, and could look forward to a hero's welcome at Yathrib, which was not far off. At two days from their journey's end, they rested in the valley of Badr. After refreshing themselves at the wells of Badr, they offered their heartfelt prayers of thanks.

The landscape began to change gradually as Yathrib drew nearer. There were more little valleys and more green orchards of palm trees. At length, Yathrib appeared on the horizon, green and wrapped in the warmth of a summer mid morning. But it wasn't until the noon of the day that the Prophet reached the southern end of the city, a suburb called Qubā'. The sight of the city brought back, into the forefront of his mind, memories of the past, memories of the journey with his mother when, at the tender age of six, he saw the grave of his father for the first time. Little had he known, while his tender heart was grieving the loss of his father, whom he had never seen, that he was soon to lose his mother. The noble parents of the Prophet are both entombed on the road to Yathrib. Other memories too must have come back to him – of former trips to Syria, the first with the much loved Abū Ṭālib, and the second when he was in charge of Khadījah's merchandise, whom he was later to marry.

A HERO'S WELCOME IN YATHRIB

No doubt because of the three days spent in the cave, the Prophet's arrival was, for his expectant followers in Yathrib, long overdue. Crowds of chieftains, of men, women and children, had been gathering on the outskirts of the city ever since news of his setting out from Makka had reached them. There were companies of riders in full armour and with colourful decorations. The Prophet, upon him be peace, is reported to have been well pleased with this reception and was all smiles and happy courtesy. He returned their greetings with equal warmth. The atmosphere was gay as for a festival: women cheered from balconies and little children lined the streets and ran along with the advancing procession.

Unauthenticated tradition has it that the crowds sang as the procession moved forward. The following is a rendering of an

Arabic ballad, still very much alive, and sung on the occasion when the Prophet's Hijra is celebrated – in it, the Prophet Muhammad's coming is compared to that of the moon:

> Through the branches of the palm trees
> that stand at the gates of the city,
> the Moon has shone upon us.
> Are we not bound to give thanks
> when a caller unto God appears?
> O you that have been sent unto us,
> that bring us honourable decree,
> You that bring honour to our city,
> Welcome! Welcome! Welcome!
> You the best of all callers.

THE PROPHET'S SHORT STAY IN QUBĀ'

Having set out from the cave on the 4th of Rabī' al-Awwal, the first year AH, the Prophet, upon him be peace, and his party reached Yathrib on the 12th of Rabī' al-Awwal. Thus he spent eight days out on the road. The normal time for that journey was eleven days. The Prophet, upon him be peace, stopped in the suburb of Qubā', two miles south of Yathrib. Quite possibly he wanted to give himself some time to assess the situation in the heart of the city. When everything was right in his judgement, he went on to the centre of the city, having spent altogether four days with the clan of Banū 'Awf in Qubā'. It is in Qubā' that the Prophet founded the very first Islamic mosque. It still exists as the Mosque of Qubā'. The Qur'ān highly commends that first Mosque because it was built on the foundation of piety and fear of God:

> ... A mosque that was founded upon God-fearing from the first day is worthier for you to stand therein; in it are men who love to purify themselves and God loves those who purify themselves. (al-Tawbah, 9: 108)

The Hypocrites, later on, established another mosque with the intention of dividing the Muslim community. The Qur'ān forbade the Prophet to pray in the Hypocrites' mosque, which was termed 'Masjid al-Ḍirār', the mosque of dissension and discord.

During his stay in Qubā', the Prophet was the guest of a

prominent Awsite by the name of Kulthūm. However, he would stay in the daytime with another Awsite Companion, called Sa'd ibn Khaythamah. Arab etiquette regarded hospitality to a worthy guest as an honour for the host, an honour to be vied for, and in no sense an imposition. The Prophet, upon him be peace, himself Arab, was familiar with such customs and must have been at great pains not to offend. Consequently, he observed every courtesy meticulously. Another consideration that made the Prophet, upon him be peace, divide his stay between Kulthūm and Khaythamah was that Khaythamah was unmarried, and could and did play host to the unmarried Muhajirs. Thus Khaythamah's house was a kind of assembly place for the Muslims. As for Abū Bakr, he was put up by another prominent Ansari Muslim, Khārijah ibn Zayd, in the neighbouring Yathrib suburb of al-Sunḥ. His stay must have been more than comfortable, for he quickly became a member of the family, through marriage to one of Khārijah's daughters.

On the 4th day, a Friday, after their arrival in the southern suburb of Yathrib (now renamed al-Madina) the Prophet and his party set out towards the centre of the city. Conditions in the city were deemed quite favourable for the Prophet's reception – in particular, there no longer seemed to be any possibility of threat to the safety of his person. The gay rejoicing and colourful celebrations that had marked the Prophet's entry into Qubā' four days before were repeated on an even more magnificent scale. Almost the whole city participated in the joyful procession that extended for almost two miles. Women stood on balconies and children climbed the roofs and trees to catch a glimpse of the Prophet's gracious and radiant presence; and they cried aloud:

> The Messenger of God has come!
> The Messenger of God has come!

Part Two

THE PROPHET'S STATE IN MADINA

4

Settling Down in Yathrib

FIRST DAYS IN QUBĀ', YATHRIB

We have seen that before going on to the quarters of his maternal uncles of Banū al-Najjār in the city, the Prophet, upon him be peace, halted at the outlying village of Qubā'. The sources differ as to the exact duration of his stay there. We have quoted Ibn Hishām who puts it at only four nights – from the Monday to the Friday. However, al-Bukhārī, in an authentic Hadith, says the Prophet's stay in Qubā' was for fourteen days.

During this stay there were many claims upon the Prophet's time. First, he received his Companions, from among both Ansar and Muhajirs: all were eager to meet him, to hear him tell the story of his dramatic and difficult escape from Makka, and his journey to Madina, and to behold once more, or for the first time, his beloved countenance. Second, after careful attention to the intelligence his hosts and visitors brought him, the Prophet had to assess the situation in Yathrib and ponder the problems and risks involved in moving there. Third, he undertook to build a mosque in Qubā', the first ever to be built, and so highly praised in the Qur'ān.[1]

Ali caught up with the Prophet in Qubā' and stayed with him in the house of Kulthūm ibn al-Hidm. It must have taken him some days to reach Qubā', since he stayed in Makka for three days after the Prophet, upon him be peace, had left. Furthermore, we know that he stayed for at least two nights in Qubā' with the Prophet. This fact is easily inferred from the incident of the single Muslim woman and her nightly visitor: Ali made enquiries about it and the woman told how Sahl ibn Ḥunayf would steal, by night, the idols of his people, destroy them and then hide them in her house.

[1] al-Tawbah, 9: 108 (see p.41).

Putting this together with the known activities of the Prophet in Qubā', it seems to us safe to accept the version of al-Bukhārī – that the Prophet, upon him be peace, stayed at Qubā' for fourteen days.

Among the Companions who hurried to meet the Prophet in Qubā' were, we may suppose, Ḥamzah, 'Umar ibn al-Khaṭṭāb, 'Ammār ibn Yāsir, Bilāl ibn Rabāh, Mas'ab ibn 'Umayr, the first Muslim envoy to Yathrib, Ibn Umm Maktūm (the blind Companion of the Surah al-A'mā (or 'Abasa), the Surah of the blind man) and Sa'd ibn Abū Waqqāṣ. All of these were Muhajirs who reached Yathrib before the Prophet. We may also safely suppose that the twelve *Nuqabā'* of the second 'Aqaba pledge were there to receive the Prophet, together with the leading men of Aws and Khazraj. Both Sa'd ibn 'Ubādah, leader of Banū Sā'idah of the Khazraj, and Usayd ibn Ḥuḍayr, one of the chief leaders of the Aws, were among the twelve *Nuqabā'*. The celebrated Sa'd ibn Mu'ādh, leader of the Aws, was not, however, a *Naqīb,* although his conversion to Islam brought in its wake a mass conversion of Yathribites to Islam. Chivalrous and very popular, he was in the forefront of the Ansar effort to uphold the cause of Islam in Madina.

The Prophet's short stay at Qubā' was a very pleasant one, resonant with joy and festivity. For the first time in over thirteen years, he felt safe and unthreatened.

ENTERING THE CITY: THE HOUSE OF ABŪ AYYŪB

After he was certain that all was well in Madina, the Prophet set out from Qubā' to the centre of the city. It was a Friday, the congregational prayer was performed for the first time in Yathrib, in the valley of the Rānūnā', crossed on the march to the city. As the procession pressed on, leading personages from Madina came forward and asked the Prophet to alight in their midst. But the Prophet tactfully apologised, saying that his famous she-camel, al-Qaswā', was commanded. Among those who approached the Prophet in this way were, according to the account of Ibn Kathīr, a group of the clan of Banū Sālim (Khazraj), including the two prominent Ansar, 'Itbān ibn Mālik and al-'Abbās ibn 'Ubādah ibn Naḍlah. They invited the Prophet to alight amongst them 'in strength, safety and wealth'. But the Prophet courteously apologised, saying that his she-camel, al-Qaswā', was commanded. Then the procession was halted by a group of Banū Bayāḍah (Khazraj),including Ziyād ibn Labīd and Farwah ibn 'Amr: the Prophet apologised as before. When the procession reached the houses of Banū al-Ḥārith (Khazraj), a large company of their men halted it and warmly invited the Prophet to alight with them. This company included several well-known men – Sa'd ibn al-Rabī' (who was host to 'Abd al-Raḥmān ibn 'Awf, and had offered him half of his wealth; Khārijah ibn Zayd (host to Abū Bakr, and since recently his father-in-law); and 'Abdullah ibn Rawāḥah (host to Bilāl, and one of the Prophet's poets). The Prophet refused as before and made the same apology.

Finally the procession reached the quarters of Banū al-Najjār, maternal uncles of the Prophet, and first of all the quarters of Banū 'Adī ibn al-Najjār, a sub-clan of Banū al-Najjār. Here too, the Prophet was invited to stay, on behalf of all, by Salīṭ ibn Qays and Abū Sulayṭ Usayrah ibn Abū Khārijah. Again the Prophet made his apology and the procession moved on.

When they reached Banū Mālik, another sub-clan of Banū al-Najjār, al-Qaswā' (the Prophet's she-camel) halted in the middle of a large and open plot of land, and sat down. The nearest dwelling was that of Abū Ayyūb, who stepped forward and invited the Prophet, pointing to his two-storey house, only a few yards away. The Prophet and Abū Bakr, having alighted from al-Qaswā', accepted the invitation and Abū Ayyūb lost no time in moving their luggage into his house. A neighbour, the celebrated As'ad ibn Zurārah, who was one of the very first Yathribites to accept Islam, came forward and led al-Qaswā' into the courtyard of his house, to take care of her for the Prophet. In this way, the problem of the Prophet's stay in Madina was settled without creating any feeling of favour or disfavour amongst the various clans of Yathrib, to whom playing host to any guest, let alone the Prophet, was a high honour capable of arousing much jealousy and competition.

For the moment, the Prophet's attention was fixed upon the large and central plot of land. He was told that it belonged to two orphan lads under the custodianship of none other than As'ad ibn Zurārah. When the Prophet disclosed his intention of building a mosque there, As'ad declared his readiness to get the land. But the Prophet insisted on paying its price, and the deal was concluded. Within a few days, the building of the mosque was enthusiastically initiated, the Prophet himself taking an active part.

The Prophet and his Companion, Abū Bakr, occupied the ground floor of Abū Ayyūb's house, while he and his wife occupied the upper floor – not without embarrassment for them to be over the head of the Prophet. Abū Ayyūb expressed this embarrassment to the Prophet, who dismissed it with a friendly, gentle smile, saying: 'O Abū Ayyūb, the ground floor is more convenient for us and for our guests.' Of these guests, there must have been a veritable flood. During the processional entry into the city, people had difficulty in distinguishing the Prophet from Abū Bakr and kept asking which of the two men was the Prophet. In particular, the women singers of Banū al-Najjār were anxious to catch a glimpse of the Prophet's face. Inevitably, those unable to see him when he entered the city flocked to Abū Ayyūb's house to satisfy their passionate curiosity, and the excitement in the streets was far from over. Echoes of the melodious voices of the young maidens of Banū al-Najjār, who regarded the Prophet (because he was a blood relative) as their very own, filled every corner of Yathrib. The living presence of the highest human ideals, of bright hopes amid music and joy, the enormous outpouring of shared affection for the person of Muhammad, Prophet of the One, True God, made the Yathrib of this time an all but supernaturally happy city. We readily imagine what gratitude, what exquisite certainty of having been blessed, moved the hearts of the singers who claimed: 'We are young maidens of Banū al-Najjār. How wonderful is Muhammad when he stands by us as a neighbour!' And we may recall once more that lovely tribute to the radiance of the Prophet of God:

The moon has shone bright upon us
Through the branches of the palm trees!
Standing at the gates of the city!
Grateful, grateful must we be
Whenever a caller unto God appears.
O ye that have been sent unto us

You've come with most welcome decree!
You have come to honour the city.
Welcome! Welcome!
You most welcome of all callers.

Those sounds are still echoed in the streets of Madina, making it one of the most cherished spots on earth, a second Makka towards which millions of hearts turn with love and adoration.

Abū Ayyūb's house was, inevitably, the centre of all the attention and emotion that the Prophet's presence attracted, and it remained so for the full seven months of his stay. The house was also honoured by being, for that seven months, the focus of the Divine revelations to the Prophet: thus the name of Abū Ayyūb has become universally known, universally honoured.

Abū Ayyūb and his wife were delighted with their guest. As is the Arabian custom, the duties of hospitality were shared with neighbours and, each evening, three or four would come, with dinner in their hands and, in their eyes, a shining look expressive of their desire to serve the Prophet, upon him be peace. Only two anxious moments marred the contentment of the hosts. The first was when a pot of water broke and a great deal of water spilled onto the floor. Afraid that it might drip down to the floor below, Abū Ayyūb used the whole of his bed sheet in an attempt to mop it up. Then he went down to the Prophet and entreated yet again that he move to the upper floor. Seeing his distraught condition, the Prophet this time agreed.

The second anxious moment was when the Prophet, upon him be peace, returned the food that had been prepared for him, untouched. Abū Ayyūb rushed upstairs, profoundly disturbed, and asked: 'O Prophet of God, did you not like our food tonight?' And the Prophet explained, 'O no, Abū Ayyūb. But I found in it the strong smell of garlic and onions. You may eat it, if you wish; but I speak to one to whom you do not speak.'[2] He referred to the Angel Gabriel.

Abū Ayyūb was greatly cherished by Muslims for the particular care he took of the Prophet. 'Abdullah ibn 'Abbās had

[2] Muslim.

a chance of honouring Abū Ayyūb when he visited him in Iraq, where he was governor for Alī ibn Abū Ṭālib. Ibn 'Abbās was at that time the governor of al-Baṣrah: to show his high regard for Abū Ayyūb, he vacated his home and insisted on putting him up there for the duration of his stay. The house of Abū Ayyūb was bequeathed by him to his freed-man and ultimately bought by a rich Muslim who gave it as a gift to a poor Muslim family.

BRINGING THE PROPHET'S FAMILY FROM MAKKA

Quite naturally, some weeks after settling in Abū Ayyūb's house the Prophet began to think of his family in Makka. He sent Zayd ibn Hārithah, his close friend and confidant, to Makka to fetch them. There were his wife, Sawdah, and his two daughters Fāṭimah and Umm Kulthūm. Under the instigation of Abū Lahab, her father-in-law, and in order to hurt the Prophet, Umm Kulthūm had been divorced by her unbelieving husband. Zayd, who was accompanied by an aide, Abū Rāfi', and given a handsome purse of about five hundred dirhams, was also entrusted with bringing back Abū Bakr's family, as well as his own family, likewise left behind in Makka. It should be remembered that Zayd's family were never apart from the Prophet's. For this reason, Zayd (a former Syrian slave), his wife Barakah (an Abyssinian) and their son Usāmah were bound to the Prophet by the strongest ties of mutual affection. Zayd was termed *'Ḥibb Rasūl Allāh',* the much-loved friend of the Prophet; similarly, his son Usāmah was called *'Ḥibb Rasūl Allāh wa ibn ḥibbihī'* (the love of the Messenger of God and the son of his love). Barakah, better known as Umm Ayman, was the Prophet's childhood nurse and governess, and her son Ayman (from a man other than Zayd) had been his childhood playmate. Thus, the house of Zayd were in every sense part of the Prophet's own – as were indeed some others, like Salmān the Persian.

Zayd and Abū Rāfi' were able to travel in safety to Makka and apparently met no hostility or opposition from the Quraysh. It would seem that the Quraysh had not as yet woken up to the full implications of the Prophet's successful Hijra. When Zayd got to Makka, only a few weeks had passed since the Hijra. The Quraysh had not yet quite recovered from the psychological shock of failing to prevent the Prophet's departure from Makka. That this must be the case is borne out by their treatment of the Prophet's daughter, Zaynab, when she tried to leave Makka much later, and who was almost killed by the Quraysh. The difference in their treatment of various members of the Prophet's family cannot be explained by the supposition that the Quraysh attitude towards them was anything other than utter hostility and opposition. Maltreatment of the Muslims, including the Prophet's own family, was the rule rather than the exception. Thus, they should not be given any credit for sparing Fāṭimah and Umm Kulthūm, only a few weeks after an abortive attempt on the life of their father. Perhaps they did not wish to provoke a new row with the Prophet, now that he had left their city and established himself elsewhere. It is safer to suppose that, at that juncture in their war with Islam, the Quraysh attitude was essentially that of one who sits on the fence – of wait-and-see. The initiative obviously lay with the Prophet, far away in Madina.

The two guides left the city of Makka quietly. With them was Sawdah, the Prophet's wife, one of the early Muslims who migrated to Abyssinia. Her first husband died there and the Prophet married her, it seems, from compassion and in appreciation of her role in the early days of his message. Having married her in Makka after the death of Khadījah, she remained his sole wife for almost four years and until he married 'Ā'ishah, some seven or eight months after his Hijra. Sawdah was rather advanced in years, although we do not know exactly how old she was at the time of her marriage to the Prophet. Then there was Faṭimah, beloved daughter of the Prophet and who resembled him the most in her appearance. Umm Kulthūm had recently been divorced and was living in her father's house at the time of the Hijra. Only Zaynab was left behind with her unbelieving husband, the gentle al-'Āṣ ibn al-Rabī'. Ruqayyah, the fourth daughter of the Prophet, was still in Abyssinia with her immigrant husband, 'Uthmān ibn 'Affān, who later became the third Rightly-Guided Caliph, succeeding 'Umar.

Of Abū Bakr's immediate family there were his wife, Umm

Rūmān, and 'Ā'ishah, Asmā' and 'Abdullah; also, his cousin and son-in-law, Ṭalḥah, with his wife, Umm Kulthūm, another daughter of Abū Bakr. Then there was the family of Zayd ibn Hārithah, as we have seen. So it was a sizeable group that set out towards Yathrib, the new haven for the Muslims. Arriving there, Sawdah and the Prophet's daughters joined him in Abū Ayyūb's house – but not for long, as the building of the Mosque and the Prophet's apartments were now well under way. Abū Bakr's family joined him in al-Sunḥ, where he was settled with his new father-in-law, Khārijah ibn Zayd (Khazraj). Zayd and his family, because of their intimate relationship with the Prophet's house, may have settled near him – possibly with As'ad ibn Zurārah, who lived next door. An alternative view is that he shared an apartment with Ḥamza, his formal brother according to the brotherhood scheme set up by the Prophet. But this view is doubtful as Ḥamzah was himself a Muhajir, and the sources are ambiguous as to where he took up residence in Madina. Some sources have it that Ḥamzah put up with As'ad ibn Zurārah: in this case the two possibilities suggested above become only a single possibility. However, other sources say that Ḥamzah put up with Abū Husayn.

BUILDING THE PROPHET'S MOSQUE

The construction of the Prophet's Mosque in Madina was begun almost immediately after his arrival there. It was built on the very same plot of land upon which al-Qaswā', the Prophet's camel, had stopped. The plot was immediately bought and work started. The first job was to level the ground and remove some old graves of the Yathrib polytheists. Some palm trees were removed and some thorny shrubs cleared. Then the construction of the mosque and two apartments for the Prophet's wives began. One apartment was meant for Sawdah, the other for 'Ā'ishah whose marriage to the Prophet was then quite imminent. The mosque which the Prophet and his Companions built in Madina stood on the same spot as the green-domed Great Mosque of the present time. The present mosque was enlarged and remodelled many times by successive Muslim governors of Madina. Originally the Prophet's private apartments lay outside the mosque and their doors opened onto the courtyard of the mosque. This arrangement was later modified and these apartments were incorporated in the mosque. The Prophet is buried in 'Ā'ishah's apartment with Abū Bakr and 'Umar alongside him. The most recent enlargements of the mosque were effected by the late Saudi Arabian kings, Sa'ūd and Fayṣal. Before these recent Saudi modifications, the Ottoman Turks had left their imprint on the sacred building.

The original structure which the Prophet himself designed was quite simple. He personally took part in the building process, carrying bricks and earth. As he laboured with his Companions, the Prophet, upon him be peace, would say:

> O Lord, there is no living except that of the Hereafter.
> So help the Ansar and the Muhajirs.
>
> O Lord, there is no good, excepting that of the Hereafter.
> So help (O Lord) the Ansar and the Muhajirs.

The Prophet's personal participation in the actual building did a great deal to press home to the Muslims the central importance of the mosque in the life of the Muslim community. It also helped to intensify their efforts and their enthusiasm. So, the Muslims would say: 'If we sit down whilst the Prophet labours, this will become a misguided enterprise.' A prominent Companion of the Prophet, 'Ammār ibn Yāsir, distinguished himself by his excessive zeal and industry in carrying the necessary materials. The Prophet one day saw him carry twice the load carried by the others; he looked at him most compassionately, and said: 'Oh 'Ammār, you will be killed by the rebellious group'. This prophecy was realised when 'Ammār was killed, some thirty years later, by the soldiers of Mu'āwiyah ibn Abū Sufyān – 'Ammār was fighting at the side of 'Alī ibn Abū Ṭālib in the battle of Ṣiffin.

The final building was of grey mud bricks supported on columns made from the trunks of date trees and roofed with branches of the same. The floor was covered with ordinary earth and the roof, a very feeble structure, leaked in the rain. Ibn Kathīr narrates that the Prophet directed the Muslims to build the mosque so as to resemble that built by Moses. In particular, its roof was to be a thatch of wood and branches of date trees, just as the thatching of Moses'.

Though of quite humble structure, as we have seen, the Prophet's Mosque has a glorious place in the history of Islam. It witnessed the Prophet's congregational prayers and his recitation of the Qur'ān on many an evening and morning. It witnessed the descent of the Archangel Gabriel with Divine revelations that had the most profound impact on the life of the Muslims, transforming it in every dimension. The earth was blessed and the land made holy, and the Muslims honoured, by God's last call unto the human race. The Mosque witnessed great assemblies of peace, war and victories. The remembrance of God, and the sounds of the Qur'ān, were echoed again and again by its humble walls. God's final blessings and His guidance for man were completed and perfected therein. There, the Prophet, upon him be peace, received or dispatched emissaries, received delegates and deputations offering their submission to God and to His word, and paying homage to the Prophet. Students of the Qur'ānic wisdom all but lived there day and night, and Muhajirs discussed their plans and shared their experiences and tales of far-away lands. Ascetics of every persuasion, in particular *Ahl al-Ṣuffah* (the people of the platform) spent all their time there, studying and learning and spreading the message of Islam. When Jihad was called for, they were ready to respond to the call within a few hours, being free of the petty concerns of life and, being unmarried, free of dependants.

There is some disagreement as to whether the Prophet's Mosque is the mosque referred to in the Qur'ān as 'the mosque founded on piety and godfearing from the first day' or whether that refers to the mosque of Qubā'. We have maintained that it is the latter. Indeed, this is the view held by most of our sources, although Ibn Kathīr and others are inclined towards the view that it is the former. Be that as it may, the status of the Prophet's Mosque and its religious significance in Islam is second only to the sacred sanctuary of Makka. It is the second Qibla and thus the second city of Muslim Pilgrimage. The lifelong wish of thousands of Muslims around the world is to be able to visit it and see for themselves its famous green dome. Prayers in it have a special religious significance and rewards for them are supposed to be very high indeed.

Some of the most melodious of Arabic poetry, throughout

history, has been composed to express the profound sentiments inspired by the Prophet, peace be upon him, and the green-domed mosque of Madina. These have been a very influential theme in Arabic dramatic and poetic art. Such art is widely diffused in the local folklore of Muslim countries of North Africa and in Muslim lands to the east of Arabia. In Saudi Arabia itself, it is frowned upon 'by some people'. This very rich and colourful prophetic poetry is called *Adab al-Madīḥ* (the literature in praise of the Prophet).

5

Forging Ties of Social Cohesion

THE PROPHET'S MARRIAGE TO 'Ā'ISHAH

After the completion of the Prophet's Mosque and the private apartments attached to it, there was cause for celebration in the marriage of the Prophet to 'Ā'ishah, the daughter of Abū Bakr. Although quite young – she may have been aged eleven or twelve – 'Ā'ishah was remarkably mature for her age and possessed really quite extraordinary intellectual and other qualities. These qualities were tested and soon proven in her role as the Prophet's companion. Her rich contribution to public life, especially in the field of learning and, later, in the field of politics, is strong proof of both her extraordinary capacity and of her equally remarkable father's energy in educating and realising her gifts. 'Ā'ishah's sister, Asmā', played a very significant part in helping the Prophet and her father escape the pursuit of the Quraysh during the Hijra. She too was extraordinarily mature for her years – consider her courage and nerve in the light of her age – she will have been, at most, in her early teens. Asmā' was soon afterwards married to the celebrated al-Zubayr ibn al-'Awwām and her first-born was the first Muslim child by immigrants to be born in Madina after the Hijra.

An important factor in the Prophet's marriage to 'Ā'ishah was his close and intimate relationship with Abū Bakr, her father. Given his great fondness and affection for Abū Bakr, it is only natural that the Prophet should have wished to be joined with him through marriage to 'Ā'ishah. Abū Bakr was also the Prophet's principal aide, and for this reason the two were constantly together. It is perhaps pertinent to mention here that the Prophet also later married the daughter of his second principal aide, 'Umar ibn al-Khaṭṭāb. She was a widow and not known to be either young or attractive. As a matter of fact, the Prophet married her out of compassion for her father, who had been repeatedly disappointed by both Abū Bakr and 'Uthmān declining to marry her. He complained about their response to the Prophet, who both surprised and enormously delighted him by asking to marry her himself. It is also pertinent to mention that the Prophet, upon him be peace, was linked through marriage to both 'Uthmān and Alī, both of whom were married to his daughters. It is easy to accept from this that such marriages helped to enhance social bonds of brotherhood and solidarity.

We have already mentioned that Abū Bakr married the daughter of his Khazrajite host, Khārijah ibn Zayd. Other prominent Muslims amongst the Muhajirs who married upon their arrival in Madina included 'Abd al-Raḥmān ibn 'Awf and 'Umar ibn al-Khaṭṭāb. They both married from among the Ansar. The Prophet himself is not known to have married from the Ansar – perhaps to avoid creating jealousies amongst them. It must be recalled that the Prophet was always very careful not to give the impression that he was favouring one group of Ansar over the others. His decision not to choose residence with any particular clan, but to let the issue be settled by his she-camel, al-Qaswā, shows his sensitive handling of this problem.

INSTITUTION OF BROTHERHOOD AMONG MUSLIMS

With many Muslim emigrants without means of livelihood, the Prophet laid the obligation of supporting them on the Ansar. He solved this problem by instituting brotherhood between the Ansar and Muhajirs. To each Muhajir, the Prophet, upon him be peace, assigned an Ansari Muslim to act as his brother. This brotherhood was a bond more effective and substantial than blood relationship, so much so that at first the Muslim brothers used to inherit from each other. Later on, this practice was abrogated and inheritance was solely through blood relation. In most cases the brothers consisted of one from the Ansar and one from the Muhajirs. The only exception to this pattern was the Prophet himself and members of his house. The Prophet himself took Ali as his brother, and Ḥamza and Zayd ibn Hārithah were made brothers. The four of them were of course Muhajirs. Again this fact must be explained by the Prophet's unwillingness to appear to favour one clan of the Ansar above the others, knowing how sensitive they were due to their history of conflict and rivalry, especially the Aws and the Khazraj sub-clans.

The most remarkable example of solidarity among new Muslims is that between Sa'd ibn al-Rabī' and his new brother, 'Abd al-Raḥmān ibn 'Awf. Sa'd was a very rich man and had two wives. On becoming a brother to 'Abd al-Raḥmān ibn 'Awf he offered, without hesitation, to divide his whole wealth equally with him. He even, in an extravagant tribute to this new relationship, offered to divorce one of his wives so that 'Abd al-Raḥmān might marry her if he wished. The generosity of Sa'd ibn al-Rabī' was matched by the nobility of 'Abd al-Raḥmān, who adamantly refused to take advantage of the goodwill of his new brother. Having duly thanked him and prayed warmly to God to bless him, his wealth and his family, 'Abd al-Raḥmān asked to be shown the main market place. This was located in the Jewish quarter of Banū Qaynuqā'. Then, 'Abd al-Raḥmān went there and began to trade. After a short time, he not only managed to support himself, but to raise enough money to get married. The presence of 'Abd al-Raḥmān in the market place must have been an early signal of social-economic changes that were taking place as a result of the new Muslim presence there. Before the coming of the Muslims, the Jews of Banū Qaynuqā' had obviously enjoyed a virtual monopoly of trade and crafts in Madina. Given the traditional Jewish genius in commerce, the Aws and Khazraj had been no match for them. But now, the business-minded Quraysh aristocracy were there – of whom 'Abd al-Raḥmān was a good example. His presence must have indicated to the Jews of Qaynuqā' that they had, from that time on, to put up with some measure of competition from the equally trade-oriented Muhajirs.

Among the Ansar who were given a new brother to be responsible for, the following may be noted, together with the names of their Muhajir brothers:

Mu'ādh ibn Jabal	(Ansari)
Ja'far ibn Abū Ṭālib	(Muhajir)

Khārijah ibn Zayd	(Ansari)
Abū Bakr al-Ṣiddīq	(Muhajir)
'Itbān ibn Mālik	(Ansari)
'Umar ibn al-Khaṭṭāb	(Muhajir)
Sa'd ibn Mu'ādh	(Ansari)
Abū 'Ubaydah ibn al-Jarrāḥ	(Muhajir)
Sa'd ibn al-Rabī'	(Ansari)
'Abd al-Raḥmān ibn 'Awf	(Muhajir)
Salamah ibn Salamah	(Ansari)
al-Zubayr ibn al-'Awwām	(Muhajir)

Another view had it (according to Ibn Kathīr) that al-Zubayr ibn al-'Awwām – husband of Asmā', daughter of Abū Bakr, thus a relative of the Prophet who was married to Asmā''s sister – was paired with 'Abdullah ibn Mas'ūd – a Muhājir and personal attendant of the Prophet. This confirms the Prophet's policy with members or very close associates of his own household.

Aws ibn Thābit	(Ansari)
'Uthmān ibn 'Affān	(Muhajir)
Ka'b ibn Mālik	(Ansari)
Ṭalḥah ibn 'Ubayd-Allāh	(Muhajir)
Ubayy ibn Ka'b	(Ansari)
Sa'īd ibn Zayd	(husband of Fāṭimah, daughter of al-Khaṭṭāb)
Abū Ayyūb al-Anṣari	(Ansari and host of the Prophet)
Mas'ab ibn 'Umayr	(first Muslim scholar-Ambassador to Yathrib)

'Abbād ibn Bashīr	(Ansari)
Abū Hudhayfah ibn 'Utbah	(Muhajir)
Abū Hudhayfah ibn al-Yamān	(Ansari)
'Ammār ibn Yāsir	(Muhajir)
Abū Ruwāḥah 'Abdullah ibn 'Abd al-Raḥmān	(Ansari)
Bilāl ibn Rabāḥ	(Muhajir)

The Prophet, upon him be peace, was the brother and friend of all Muslims, Ansar as well as Muhajirs. We have seen that he carefully avoided taking a formal brother from any clan of the Ansar, lest this should resurrect old rivalries. However, in order to conform to the general pattern of organising the Muslims into pairs of brothers, he instituted the following brotherhood for himself and members of his house:

Muḥammad ibn 'Abdullah and
'Alī ibn Abū Ṭālib

Ḥamzah ibn 'Abd al-Muṭṭalib and
Zayd ibn Ḥārithah

'Abdullah ibn Mas'ūd and
Zubayr ibn al-'Awwām

These three pairs form an exception to the general rule of an Ansari being made a brother of a Muhajir.

A POET'S DEPICTION OF SOCIAL LIFE IN MADINA

The humane society, rich in communal life, that was gradually emerging in Madina as a result of the implementation of Islam under the leadership of the Prophet, upon him be peace, was depicted by a poet of Banū al-Najjār, a certain Abū Qays Ṣarmah ibn Anas. He composed a number of poems to show the social changes that took place under the government of the Prophet. The principal themes can be summarised as follows:

(i) The Prophet, rejected by the Quraysh, found success, happiness and companionship in Madina.

(ii) The Prophet delighted the Yathribites with Qur'ānic teaching and Qur'ānic stories about people who had lived long ago – stories such as those of Noah and Moses.

(iii) The Yathribites were only too willing to supply him with money for the maintenance of the Muslim community, and only too willing to defend him with their lives, fighting whomsoever he fought, and making peace with whomsoever he made peace.

(iv) The Islamic notion of *Tawḥīd,* that nothing but God matters, became widespread in Madina. It became the general conviction that the Divine Guidance preached by the Prophet was the best of all guidance.

(v) In one particular poem, we find Abū Qays echoing the Islamic ideas that were dominant in the early community under the Prophet's guidance. Among those ideas we find exhortations to the believers to enrich their lives by constant remembrance of God, especially in the morning and in the evening. He also gives admonitions on a number of issues such as being God-fearing, observing *Ḥalāl,* and being compassionate and fair to orphans. He also warns against any slackness in the defence of the city's boundaries.

6

Some Major Developments in Madina

A better guide to what was going on in that formative period of the Muslim society should be sought in the Qur'ān itself.

THE QUR'ĀNIC ACCOUNT

There was, among the local Yathribites, an urgent desire, almost a need, to comprehend the phenomenon of Muhammad, upon him be peace, not only as a newcomer who suddenly assumed the position of highest authority, but also as the divinely-ordained Prophet who had been belied and expelled by his own people, and but narrowly escaped assassination. The changes that the Prophet's coming effected in the patterns and attitudes of life in Yathrib were revolutionary and proved to be permanent. His presence and the message he preached raised the moral consciousness of the Ansar and inspired in them a capacity for sacrifice – the generosity and open liberality with which they received the dispossessed, homeless immigrants is a rare instance of the triumph of the noble spirit of a man over his lowly instincts and passions. The Qur'ān has reflected this spiritual triumph:

> It (war spoils) is for the poor emigrants, who were expelled from their habitations and their possessions, seeking bounty from God and (His) good pleasure (with them) and helping God and His Messenger; those are the truthful ones.
>
> And those who dwelt in the land (Yathrib) and adopted the faith before them, loved whosoever emigrated to them, not finding in their hearts any need for what they gave, and preferring others above themselves, even though poverty was their lot. And whoso is guarded from the avarice of his own soul, he is of those who prosper. (al-Ḥashr, 59: 8-9)

Only the Ansar were in a position to help the Muhajirs – to

provide them with homes and the means of earning their living. The two groups were nevertheless working as a single community, united by the common goal of Islam. At once the major instance, and a symbol, of their togetherness, was the major public project – the building of the mosque and of apartments for the Prophet and his family. Also during his brief stay in Qubā', the Prophet had built a mosque with the help of the Ansar and Muhajirs. It is this mosque that is so highly praised in the Qur'ān (al-Tawbah, 9: 108); and the congregation that prayed in that mosque of Qubā' were also commended as 'the men who love to purify themselves and God loves those who are purified'.

Ties between the groups were strengthened through public celebration – of, first of all, a number of important marriages, including that of the Prophet himself (to 'Ā'ishah and those of 'Abd al-Raḥmān ibn 'Awf and 'Umar, to mention only a few. Zubayr ibn al-'Awwām celebrated his first-born, who was also the first Muslim child born in Madina to emigrant parents. However, these celebrations were marred by many Muhajirs falling ill because of the fever-infected air of Madina. Abu Bakr, Bilāl, 'Āmir ibn Fuhayrah, all fell ill with fever. Then two prominent Muslims from amongst the Ansar died suddenly. These were none other than As'ad ibn Zurārah, the man who, more than anyone, had been instrumental in making Madina a safe refuge for the Prophet and Makkan Muslims. The second man who died was the Prophet's host at Qubā', Kulthūm ibn al-Hidm. The tongues of the Hypocrites wagged about the Prophet's coming having been a bad omen. This was perhaps the beginning of the Hypocrites' propaganda war, a war of nerves, against the Muslims. Until the birth of the child of Zubayr ibn al-'Awwām and Asmā', there had even been rumours that the Jews had charmed the Muslims, rendering them barren. These events are not explicitly recorded in the Qur'ān, but sufficiently stressed in the *Sīrah* books and the sayings of the Prophet to be given consideration.

The ordinance of Prayer and Adhān. The direction of Prayer, Qibla, was changed from Jerusalem to Makka, the second Qibla, an event that further strained the already tense relations with the Jews. On the other hand, it also ended a long period of Jewish haughtiness that the Muslims were allegedly imitating the Jews with respect to Qibla. The change served to enhance and protect the true identity of Islam as a new Divinely-revealed religion, not to be confused either with Judaism or Christianity, though, being monotheistic, much related to both of them. Before the Hijra, prayer had consisted of only two performances, one in the morning, the other in the evening. After the Hijra, the noon, the mid-noon, and night prayers were prescribed. In particular, the middle prayer was emphasised. It is generally agreed by Muslim jurists that by the middle prayer is meant the mid-noon prayer.

Tradition has it that the Prophet was thinking about an effective way of calling people to the five daily prayers, now being held in the mosque. At first, he thought of the Jewish horn or trumpet, but did not regard it as suitable. Then, he thought of using a bell, after the manner of the Christians. Again the idea did not appeal to him. Thus, for some time, the Prophet continued the practice of sending a man to call in the streets, at the top of his voice, *'al-Ṣalāt al-Jāmi'ah'* ('to public prayer'). Then, one day, a Companion by the name of 'Abdullah ibn Zayd came along and told of a strange dream which he had had the night before. In that dream, Ibn Zayd saw a man in green robes, carrying a bell. When the man in green asked Zayd what he would do with the bell, Ibn Zayd replied that he would use it for calling people to public prayers. The man in green then suggested the Adhan as it is known today:

> Greatest is Allah.
> Greatest is Allah.
> I bear witness, that there is no god but Allah.
> I bear witness that Muhammad is the Messenger of Allah.

The Prophet, upon him be peace, accepted this dream as authentic and the *Adhān* in its present form was called by Bilāl as seen in the dream of Ibn Zayd.

Some of these events are vividly reflected in the Qur'ān. For instance, the change of the Qibla gave fresh impetus to the arguments between the Muslims and the Jews, who naturally regarded the move as unsanctionable. The Qur'ān tells us that the Prophet had long been seeking an alternative Qibla but awaited Divine guidance:

> We have seen the turning of your face to heaven (for guidance). Now assuredly, We shall give you a qibla with which you will be well pleased. So turn your face towards the Ḥarām (the Inviolable House) ... (al-Baqarah, 2: 144)

To the Jews' questions about the rationale of this change, the Qur'ān (al-Baqarah, 2: 142) replied that to God belongs the East and West and that He is free to direct their prayers as He wishes:

> The weak-minded among the people will say: 'What has turned them away from the direction of prayer which they have hitherto observed'. Say: 'God's is the east and west; He guides whom He wills onto a straight way.'

The command to fast during the month of Ramaḍān was given as follows:

> O you who believe. Fasting is ordained for you, even as it was ordained for those before you, that you may fear (your Lord). (al-Baqarah, 2: 183)

When the Prophet came to Madina, he found the Jews fasting the Day of 'Āshurah (the Day of Atonement). According to Ibn Kathīr, the Prophet, learning from the Jews that it was the day on which God delivered Moses from his enemies, ordered the Muslims to observe it, saying that the Muslims were more worthy of Moses than the Jews.

This fact concerning the Day of Atonement is narrated in both Bukhārī and Muslim. The fasting of Ramaḍān and the changing of the Qibla both were prescribed in the second year of the Hijra but before the battle of Badr. According to Ibn Kathīr, the changing of the Qibla was effected in Sha'bān some eighteen months after the Hijra. He also maintains that it was quite probable that Ramaḍān was likewise prescribed in Sha'bān of the same year, i.e. the second year of the Hijra. *Zakāt* was also prescribed at approximately the same time.

THE QUR'ĀN MOBILISES THE UMMA

The Qur'ān had a powerful impact on the lives of the Madinians in the period that preceded the battle of Badr. Its impact not only radically changed their inner and outer lives, and remodelled their society, it also generated the moral and spiritual energy that was soon to transform the world. The initial phase of this burst of moral energy was, quite understandably, to be directed towards stopping the transgressions and evil of the Quraysh – the evil in particular of religious repression. The Qur'ān dealt carefully with all the issues involved in armed conflict.

It repeated the then newly-given permission to fight in self-defence. Religious repression *(al-fitnah)* was pronounced to be worse than killing, and as such a paramount evil; combating it and securing religious freedom must be given first priority. The Ḥaram of Makka (the Holy Sanctuary) was to be given due respect, but abuse of its sanctity by agents of the Quraysh was not to be permitted. If need be, neither this special sanctity of the Ḥaram, nor that of the holy Arabian months, during which, in accordance with pre-Islamic tradition, pilgrimage to the Ka'bah took place, should be allowed to stand in the way of fighting the Quraysh tyranny. Last but not least, conflict with evil and falsehood was deemed inevitable. If the Muslims failed to counter evil and falsehood, religion would be destroyed.

Although these were touched upon in the opening chapter, it is worth mentioning here some of the critical points made in the Surahs in justification of armed conflict.

The initial permission to fight given in Surah al-Ḥajj emphasises the causes and the objectives of such fighting. Fighting was instituted (a) to combat the oppression of Muslims, and their expulsion from their homes, for no reason other than their religious convictions; and (b) to prevent the destruction of the houses of God, be they synagogues, churches or mosques, until 'all religion becomes God's' – in sum, to win and establish the right of every monotheistical community to religious self-determination. The relevant verses here are those of Surah al-Ḥajj (22: 39-41).

It is interesting that verses 40 and 41 stress that the struggle against *Shirk* (polytheism) is absolutely essential if religious places of worship are to be maintained.

These verses also predict that the moment the righteous forces are victorious, they establish *Salāt, Zakāt,* and occupy themselves in reforming and organising all things related to the material and spiritual well-being of the people.

In Surah al-Baqarah, (2: 190-193), the command to fight is given important qualifications:

(a) Although fighting is, in those circumstances and with those motives, permitted, yet the Muslims are not to transgress. God does not love the transgressors.

(b) Also, the Muslims are not to initiate a fight inside the Ḥaram, the Sacred Mosque Sanctuary, of Makka. However, if the polytheists took advantage of this and tried to kill the Muslims, then they were at liberty to fight them.

(c) It is this verse that declares persecution to be worse than killing, and, once more, names the objective as the achievement of religious freedom for all monotheistic worshippers, 'until all religion becomes God's'.

In Surah Muḥammad (47: 20-21) we find a frank admission that there was a group of faint-hearted believers who hedged and hesitated, when the command to fight was received. The Qur'ān not only brought into the open their weakness and hesitation, but it sought to educate and inspire them:

> Those who believe say: If only a Surah were sent down (commanding war, then we would fight). Then when a clear Surah is sent down, and therein fighting is mentioned, you see those in whose hearts is sickness looking at you as one overshadowed with death ...

Other Qur'ānic verses allude to such issues as the importance of the contributions of Muslims to the effort and expenses of war. The Muslims are advised that the command to wage war against the tyrannic forces that seek to extinguish the light of God is meant to be a trial and a test for them. Those who pass this test will be known as sincere and strong; those who fail would invite questions about their sincerity and steadfastness. The Qur'ān reiterates that God is not unable to crush the forces of tyranny by Himself, but has decreed that there be a struggle by the Muslims against them.

Other Surahs that belong to this period take up the emergent opposition to Islam from among the Hypocrites and the Jews of Madina. These Qur'ānic verses will be dealt with below, when we discuss the phenomenon of the Hypocrites and the Jewish question.

THE PROPHET'S FIRST ENCOUNTER WITH THE JEWS

The conversion of 'Abdullah ibn Salām, a leading Rabbi among the Jews of Madina (according to Ibn Hishām), is recorded by the major sources. The Prophet's meeting with Ibn Salām was, perhaps, his first experience of the Jews of the city. Ibn Hishām says that 'Abdullah ibn Salām had collected enough information about Muhammad, upon him be peace, to recognise him as the true Arabian Prophet, foretold in the Jewish scriptures. However, Ibn Salām disclosed this to no-one. On hearing of the Prophet's arrival in Qubā', he straightaway hurried to meet him. The first glance convinced him that the Prophet's face was not the face of an imposter, and when, after a time, the Prophet had settled in the city in the house of Abū Ayyūb al-Anṣārī, Ibn Salām visited him.

Both Ibn Hishām and Ibn Kathīr give an account of that meeting. Ibn Hishām states that 'Abdullah became a Muslim after the first meeting in Qubā', but kept his conversion a close secret. When he came to see the Prophet for the second time, in Abū Ayyūb's house, he said: 'The Jews (of Madina) are a nation of liars, so please hide me in one of your rooms, call them and ask them about me, before you inform them about my conversion.' Ibn Hishām says that the Prophet did as 'Abdullah asked. When the Jews were assembled in his home, the Prophet asked them what kind of man 'Abdullah ibn Salām was. They answered that he was their master and the son of their master, and that he was one of their leading Rabbis. Then 'Abdullah stepped out of hiding and declared his acceptance of Islam and called upon them to do the same, saying that Muhammad, upon him be peace, was the Prophet foretold in the scriptures. Straightaway forgetting how highly, only a few moments before, they had valued him, the assembled Jews now called Ibn Salām a liar and heaped scorn and curses upon him. In this way, according to Ibn Hishām, Ibn Salām made his point about the attitude of the Jews of Madina. However, if this incident is authentic, it seems to have done little to prevent the Prophet from striving hard to win the Jews' support and co-operation within the commonwealth that he was setting up in Madina. If the treaty which he was able to conclude with them is a reliable guide, the Prophet did succeed in achieving a measure of co-operation and goodwill. This treaty represents the basic constitutional document on which the Prophet's commonwealth was established in Madina. In fact, it almost amounted to a system of confederated local government in which the Jews retained full control over most of their internal affairs, while the Prophet controlled and directed foreign and defence affairs. It is unrealistic to suppose that the conclusion of this document with the Jews of Madina was achieved by the Prophet without a considerable campaign to win their confidence.

Of the conversion of 'Abdullah ibn Salām, Ibn Kathīr gives two versions. The first is very much that given by Ibn Hishām. But the second mentions that Ibn Salām questioned the Prophet about three issues: (a) about signs of the approach of Doomsday; (b) about the first food to be fed to the people of Paradise; and (c) about the sex of the offspring, whether a boy or a girl. Ibn Kathīr asserts that the Prophet knew the right answers through the information he received from the Angel Gabriel. So he gave the right answers and 'Abdullah was convinced that he was the true Prophet foretold in the Jewish scriptures.

7

The Hypocrites of Madina

INTRODUCTION

What is a Munāfiq? A Hypocrite or *Munāfiq* was not known to exist during the Makkan period of Islam. The phenomenon only emerged at Madina when the victory of Islam was clear to foes as well as friends. The term munāfiq was used by the Qur'ān and Muslims to designate some of the most formidable of their adversaries. The word did not exist in the pre-Islamic Arabic vernacular. Its derogatory connotations are clear: a Munafiq is one who hesitates between two opposed groups, pretending to belong to the faction which he really opposes; typically, he does this out of expediency, the group which he really opposes being the stronger group. A Munafiq is literally someone who constantly shifts his ground so that it is very hard to lay one's hand on him.

In Makka, there had been no need for hypocrisy. Islam was weak and oppressed. Since to profess it cost a great deal of suffering, affliction and sacrifice, only genuine persons dared to do so. On the other hand, the failure to profess it brought no unfavourable consequences: the Quraysh would be gratified by it, and the Muslims too weak to censure it. The situation was otherwise in Madina. To be a Muslim was to ride the winning horse. To fail to declare oneself Muslim was to remain on the fringe of society. Since there should be no compulsion in religion, according to Islam, the question of persecuting non-Muslims did not arise. Why then were there Hypocrites, Munafiqs? These were men with a fundamental weakness of character, the inability to take a stand. A Munafiq was really opposed to the Prophet, instinctively and because of his self-interest, but too weak to disclose his real stance and his real motives. Perhaps the Munafiq feared, deep in his heart, that his stance was neither wholesome nor honourable, but self-interest and meanness of character prevented him from taking the correct, honourable stance. Thus, he resorted to hypocrisy; he would pretend to be a Muslim, a devoted follower of the Prophet, whereas he was, in reality, far from it.

WHO WERE THE MUNAFIQS?

Sources of the *Sīrah* of the Prophet are unanimous in ascribing a leading role to the Jews of Madina and to two prominent Yathribites in nursing and fostering hypocrisy in Madina. The Jews, who were initially on friendly terms with the Prophet, soon realised that they and the Muslims in Madina had divergent aims. The growth of the Prophet's authority in the city threatened the vital commercial and political interests of the Jews. Since their position of eminence in Madina was secured by these interests, the Jews naturally came to the conclusion that they must, by every means, challenge and actively resist the authority of the Prophet.

One of their strategies was to encourage disaffection amongst the native Yathribites and incite them to opposition against the Muslim rule. The Jews found two willing partners in this mischief-making. These were 'Abdullah ibn Ubayy ibn Salūl, the undisputed leader and mastermind of the Munafiqs, and a certain Abū 'Āmir ibn 'Abd 'Āmir al-Sayfī. The first man belonged to the Khazraj, but was also highly respected by the Aws. The second man, however, was of the Aws tribe. According to historical sources, up to the time of the Prophet's arrival in Madina no man, among Jews or Arabs, was more highly regarded in that city than 'Abdullah ibn Ubayy ibn Salūl. In fact, by common popular consent he was to have been crowned king of the city. Preparations had been under way for his enthronement, including the making of a special, jewelled crown. So, in a sense, his frustrations are understandable.

The second man, Ibn al-Sayfī, was foremost among the Aws. If Ibn Ubayy was aspiring to secular authority in Yathrib, Ibn al-Sayfī aspired rather to spiritual authority, in recognition of which he was called *al-Rāhib,* 'the monk'. He claimed to be of the religion of Prophet Abraham. When he learned of the advent of the Prophet in Madina, he went to him and asked what religion he followed. Upon hearing that it was the religion of Abraham, al-Sayfī became enraged and contradicted the Prophet's statement, claiming that he, al-Sayfī, was the only true follower of Abraham, and most worthy of his name and his religion. The Prophet, in turn, refuted this, at which point al-Sayfī made an invocation to the effect that whichever of the two of them was not telling the truth, let him die lonely and forlorn, a complete stranger in a far-away land. The Prophet said Amen to his invocation. Soon afterwards, al-Sayfī suddenly departed with fifteen or fifty (there are two versions to his story) of his Aws supporters and settled in Makka. The Prophet invited people to call him not a *rāhib* or monk, but a *fāsiq* or transgressor. When later on, the Prophet invaded Makka, al-Sayfī fled alone to Syria, where he died, wretched and totally isolated.

As to the unquestioned leader of the Hypocrites, 'Abdullah ibn Ubayy ibn Salūl, he chose to stay on in Madina, pretending to be a good Muslim. So he will be with us in this narrative for quite some time, at the centre of events, wherever there was hypocrisy, or mischief, against the Prophet or the Muslims. He figures prominently in virtually all the major events involving the Hypocrites and their opposition to the Prophet.

Regarding the actual number of the Hypocrites, accounts differ. Their number is given as forty-two or forty-three by Aḥmad ibn Ḥanbal in his *Musnad,* who adds that five of them later repented and became good Muslims. But a higher figure would be more realistic: it must be recalled that 'Abdullah ibn Ubayy ibn Salūl brought back a third of all the Muslim army that was on its way to the battle of Uḥud. If those who followed and then returned with him to Madina were all Hypocrites, then their number must have been closer to three hundred men. But quite clearly that number included besides the Hypocrites, the cowardly and the feeble-hearted, some of whom were no doubt Muslims, who could not be said to be Hypocrites in any way but were simply running for their lives. Perhaps the most acceptable version is that of Ibn 'Abbās, who puts the figure at between one hundred and seventy and three hundred men.

It is stated that Allah, *subbhānahū wa ta'ālā,* had revealed to His Prophet the identity of all the Hypocrites in Madina. The Prophet disclosed this information to Abū Ḥudhayfah al-Yamān, and told him to keep it a secret, a command which he obeyed absolutely. The disclosure was made after an incident involving the Prophet and Abū Ḥudhayfah. While the Prophet and his army were returning from the battle of Tabūk, a group of Hypocrites tried to ambush him at an elevated place when he had become separated from the bulk of his army. 'Ammār ibn Yāsir, the well-known Companion of the Prophet whose Yemeni father, Yāsir, and Makkan mother, Sumayyah, were the first martyrs in Islam, was leading al-Qaswā', the Prophet's she-camel, and Abū Ḥudhayfah was marching behind. When Abū Ḥudhayfah noticed the approach of the masked men, he charged at them, hitting ferociously at their camels. Realising that their assassination attempt had been foiled, the masked men fled in disarray, afraid that the nearby Muslim army might be alerted. The Prophet was pleased at the courage of Abū Ḥudhayfah, and in secret confided to him the names of the Hypocrites. In later times, when Muslims were forbidden to pray for the deceased Hypocrites, they would watch Abū Ḥudhayfah whenever a Muslim died: only if he prayed for the man would they too pray. This incident is recounted in detail by Abū Sulaymān al-Dimashqī as narrated by Imam Aḥmad in his *Musnad.*

Two types of Munāfiqs. The well-known jurist Ibn Taymīyah, as quoted by the commentator, al-Safrā'inī, of *Musnad* Aḥmad, said that Munafiqs will continue to exist until the Day of Judgement. Al-Safrā'inī also quotes al-Zamakhsharī and others on the issue of Munafiqs. He sums up by saying that Munafiqs are of two types: (i) those who commit the *nifāq* of *Kufr,* i.e. hypocrisy leading to unbelief; and (ii) those who merely commit the *nifāq* of *'amal* (hypocrisy of deed or action). The second group are not unbelievers, but insincere in their deeds. To this latter group is directed the well-known Hadith (saying) of the Prophet, upon him be peace, concerning the four marks of the Hypocrite: said the Prophet, 'There are four traits, he who has all of them is a Munafiq par excellence, and he who has one of them has some *nifāq* (hypocrisy) in him, until he gets rid of it: (a) if given a trust, he betrays it; (b) when he speaks, he lies; (c) when he promises something, he does not keep his promise; and (d) when he quarrels, he commits excesses.' (Bukhārī and Muslim.)

A second Hadith which is perhaps concerned with the first category of the Hypocrites is given by Ibn Kathīr while commenting on Surah al-Munāfiqūn (the Surah of the Hypocrites – Surah 63): narrated Aḥmad ibn Ḥanbal, on the authority of Abū Hurayrah, that the Prophet, upon him be peace, said:

> The *Munāfiq* has signs by means of which you may know him:
> i their greeting is cursing;
> ii their food is unlawfully obtained;
> iii their living is secured through unjust means *(ghalūl)*, doing wrong and injustice to others;
> iv they do not approach mosques except occasionally;
> v they do not attend prayer, except in the very last rows;
> vi they are an arrogant lot, disinclined towards fellow Muslims, and Muslims are not inclined towards them;
> vii they sleep like logs during the night, but are noisy during the day.

PROMINENT HYPOCRITES

The following account of some prominent Hypocrites is based on Ibn Hishām. Of the two leading figures of the Hypocrites, Ibn al-Sayfī died an outcast in Syria, as we have seen. Of Ibn Ubayy ibn Salūl a full account will be given subsequently. The following are the names and some accounts of other prominent figures in the Hypocrite movement – prominent in the sense that they had committed some major mischief against the Prophet and against the Muslims and that their mischief is alluded to in the Qur'ān.

Julās (or Jilās) ibn Suwayd ibn al-Ṣāmit. Having failed to join the Prophet at the battle of Tabūk, Julās said, 'If the Prophet is right about what he is doing (an allusion to the war at Tabūk), then we are worse than asses.' This statement is referred to in the Qur'ān (al-Tawbah, 9: 74) as the world of *Kufr* (unbelief). Sitting with him at the time in which he uttered the above statement was his adopted son 'Umayr ibn Sa'd. Julās married 'Umayr's mother after his father died. 'Umayr was young and an enthusiastic Muslim. He also loved Julās as a father. 'Umayr's predicament was therefore the following: (i) if he told the Prophet, then his adoptive father would be in grave trouble; (ii) but if he kept silent, then he would be betraying his religion. He decided not to betray his religion. He disclosed this decision in a moving apology to his father and went straight to the Prophet and told him about Julās' unfortunate statement. It is related that Julās repented later on, and in his last days was accepted by the believers as a good Muslim. Three others, also reported to have repented and become good Muslims in their later days, are Ka'b ibn Mālik, Abū Lubābah, and Mukhashshin ibn Ḥumayyar.

Al-Ḥārith ibn Suwayd ibn al-Ṣāmit. Brother of Julās, he killed a Muslim (with whom he had had a blood feud since pre-Islamic times) during the battle of Uḥud, and fled to Makka. The Muslims declared that he was wanted for murder, and 'Umar vowed to kill him next time he met him. Pleas for his pardon from his brother Julās were not accepted.

Nabtal ibn al-Ḥārith. He was a very big, ugly man, darkish red in complexion, with long untidy hair. His eyes were as red as two spots of copper. He would attend the Prophet's lectures and sermons, then jest and joke about them. He would say that Muhammad was all ears, meaning that he was too willing to listen to his guests. The Qur'ān condemned him as a Hypocrite and as Satan-like, both in his ways and his looks.

Tha'labah ibn Ḥāṭib, Mu'attib ibn Qushayr, Jāriyah ibn 'Āmir ibn al-'Attāf and his two sons, *Zayd* and *Mujamma'*. They all shared in the building of the Masjid al-Ḍirār or splinter group mosque. Although a rival to the Prophet's mosque, the Prophet was willing at first to tolerate it. However, after God revealed to him the Hypocrites' ultimate intentions, he ordered it burnt and destroyed. The Qur'ān condemned the builders of the Ḍirār Mosque, whose full story will be told below. Tha'labah ibn Ḥāṭib and Mu'attib ibn Qushayr later repented and became good Muslims.

Wadī'ah ibn Thābit. He was another of the builders of Masjid al-Ḍirār. When rebuked about it, he replied that he had only been joking. But the Qur'ān condemned him squarely for it (al-Tawbah, 9: 65).

Khidhām ibn Khālid. He gave his horse to help in the construction of the Masjid al-Ḍirār.

Mirbi' ibn al-Qayzī. He was an old and blind man through whose orchard the Prophet had to go to get to the battlefield. The man was infuriated and threatened to throw a handful of mud and clay at the Prophet. The Companions leapt upon him, one of them striking Mirbi' on the head with an arrow. They would surely have killed him, but the Prophet ordered them to leave him alone, saying he was blind both in his vision and his heart.

Aws ibn al-Qayzī. The brother of Mirbi', he obtained permission from the Prophet not to take part in the battle of the Ditch, saying his house was insecure. He was condemned in the Qur'ān and portrayed as a coward, who desired to flee the war (al-Aḥzāb, 33: 137).

There were many others, some of whom had Jewish backgrounds, but the forementioned names are sufficient to give an insight into what sort of men those Hypocrites were. However, this account would be most incomplete without 'Abdullah ibn Ubayy ibn Salūl, their leader, and the most outspoken and daring amongst them.

'ABDULLAH IBN UBAYY IBN SALŪL

Most authorities agree that the greater part of Surah al-Munāfiqūn (63) was revealed on 'Abdullah ibn Ubayy, but, without doubt, this Qur'ānic portrait of a Munafiq is meant to be general as well:

> When the hypocrites come to you, they say, We bear witness that you are indeed the Messenger of God. And God knows that you are indeed His Messenger, but God bears witness that the hypocrites are in fact liars.
>
> They make their oaths a protection, then they turn back from the way of God. Surely they have been doing evil things. That is because they believed, then they have disbelieved, therefore a seal has been imprinted on their hearts, and (so) they do not understand.
>
> When you see them, their appearance pleases you; and when they speak, you listen to their speech, but it is as if they were

> propped up timbers. They think every calamity is upon them. They are the enemy, so beware of them, the curse of God upon them how they are perverted! (verses 1-4)

All these traits of the Hypocrites, mentioned in the above verses, were particularly true in the case of Ibn Ubayy ibn Salūl. Whenever he met the Prophet, he was especially noisy about being a good Muslim, and would make every effort to show the Prophet that he believed in his Prophethood. But, as soon as he was with his fellow Hypocrites, he would deny that belief, thus confirming himself in falsehood and unbelief.

The Prophet visits Ibn Ubayy. One day, the Prophet, upon him be peace, was on his way to visit a sick Companion of his, Sa'd ibn 'Ubādah, the chief of the Khazraj. On the way, he passed by the house of Ibn Ubayy, and thought it would be courteous and becoming to call upon him, and did so. The Prophet, being admitted, sat in the house of Ibn Ubayy and recited some portions of the Qur'ān, and delivered a brief sermon. Ibn Ubayy remarked that the sermon was very fine but that it would have been better for the Prophet to deliver it at home – in that way, those interested in listening to him could go there, and those not inclined to listen would be spared. The unkind and unpleasant implications of these discourteous words were not lost upon the Muslims present. They immediately contradicted Ibn Ubayy and assured the Prophet that he was indeed most welcome to preach wherever he liked. Despite this sincere assurance by the other Muslims, the gracious Prophet, being himself very delicate in such matters of courtesy, was deeply grieved at the insensitive and unjust affront given him by Ibn Ubayy. That grief persisted and was visible on his face when he entered the house of Sa'd ibn 'Ubādah, who, used to seeing the Prophet in good humour and high spirits, could not help but ask if something had displeased him.

The eviction of Ibn Ubayy from the Prophet's Mosque. Nor was that the only occasion on which Ibn Ubayy caused sadness and dismay among the Muslims. While the Muslims were marching to meet the enemy at Uḥud, Ibn Ubayy persuaded a third of the men to go back with him to Madina. Now, it was his habit to speak to the congregation at the Prophet's Mosque every Friday. He would stand up just before the Prophet himself did to deliver his sermon, and say:

> O people! This is the Prophet of God amongst you. Indeed God has honoured you in him and made you victorious by his presence amidst you. So listen carefully to what he has to say and do not fail to obey him.

After the Prophet's return from Uḥud, Ibn Ubayy stood up to speak as usual, undeterred by what he had done. But a group of Muslims pulled his mantle and shouted him down, saying:

> 'O enemy of God, sit down. You are not worthy of that stance or of those words, after doing what you did at Uḥud.'

But instead of sitting down, Ibn Ubayy angrily made for the door of the mosque, muttering, 'As if I had done something evil in standing up to support him (meaning the Prophet).' At the door of the mosque, some Muslims entreated Ibn Ubayy to go back and ask the Prophet to forgive him. But he adamantly refused to do so. A verse of Surah al-Munāfiqūn refers to this incident as follows:

> And when it is said to them, 'Come now and God's messenger will ask forgiveness for you', they twist their heads, and you see them turning their faces away, waxing proud. (verse 63: 5)

Ibn Ubayy ibn Salūl and his son. When the Muslim forces were returning to Madina after the battle of Banū al-Musṭalaq, a petty quarrel developed between a Muslim of the Ansar and another of the Muhajirs. Each of them shouted to his group for help. The small incident threatened to involve the whole army and grow into a tragic conflict amongst the Muslims. When Ibn Ubayy heard of the incident, he was enraged and said: 'It serves us right. We have given refuge to these vagabonds of the Quraysh (referring to the Muhajirs by the hateful nickname of al-Țalābib) and now they vie with us and even fight us. Nothing describes our situation so well as the Arab proverb 'Fatten your dog and it will eat you'. Then he vowed that on his return to Madina 'the stronger would drive out the weaker'. Zayd ibn Arqam, a young Muslim, heard this vow of Ibn Ubayy's and told the Prophet. The Prophet ordered an immediate march of the army. He made the Muslims march the rest of that day, the whole of the night, and the next morning until it was too hot for them to continue. Then he ordered a halt. As soon as they stepped down from their camels the Muslims fell asleep from exhaustion and fatigue. This was precisely the aim of the Prophet – that the Muslims should have no energy left to revive the quarrel. Then, the Prophet summoned Ibn Ubayy and asked him about his vow as related to him by Zayd. Ibn Ubayy swore that he had not said it. Some Muslims supported him and urged the Prophet not to rely on the evidence of a small boy, namely, Zayd ibn Arqam. But God revealed to His Prophet the truth about the whole matter: Zayd was vindicated and Ibn Ubayy incriminated and condemned. The Companions called for the punishment of Ibn Ubayy. His own son, 'Abdullah ibn 'Abdullah ibn Ubayy, who was a good Muslim, came to the Prophet and volunteered to kill his father, if that was the wish of the Prophet. But the gracious Prophet showed only kindness and compassion. 'No, no!' he said, 'we shall not kill your father. On the contrary, we shall be kind and charitable towards him, as long as he stays with us. By God, I would not have the Arabs saying that Muhammad kills his own companions.'

Needless to say, 'Abdullah ibn 'Abdullah ibn Ubayy, who naturally loved his father, was greatly impressed and relieved. But he was determined to teach his father a lesson. He hurried to the gate of the city of Madina and stood there, his sword in hand. When his father came to the gate to enter the city, he prevented him, saying, 'Today we are going to see who is the stronger and who is the weaker. By God, you will not be allowed to enter until the Prophet gives you permission to do so. The Prophet was way behind. So Ibn Ubayy had to wait, till the Prophet came to the gate. 'He will not be allowed to enter, unless you say so, Prophet of Allah' said the son of Ubayy ibn Salūl. But the Prophet readily gave Ibn Ubayy permission to enter and he did so, feeling humbled and humiliated.

Ibn Ubayy ibn Salūl and the affair of Ifk. This incident of the quarrel between Ansar and Muhajirs and Ibn Ubayy's subsequent humiliation apparently did not succeed in convincing him to give up his hypocrisy and start behaving himself as a good Muslim. He was soon to become involved in the scandalous affair of the *Ifk,* in which the Prophet's wife 'Ā'ishah was unjustly accused. An account of this will be given below; we note his involvement here to illustrate the point that in the case of many of the Munafiqs, certainly in the case of Ibn Ubayy, 'hypocrisy' was almost pathologically wilful – he could not help himself, such was his blindness. The Qur'ān comments:

> 'They say, if we return to Madina the mightier ones will expel the lowlier; yet Glory belongs unto God, and unto His Messenger and the believers, but the hypocrites do not know it.'(al-Munāfiqūn, 63: 8)

THE PROPHET DEALS WITH THE HYPOCRITES

Extent of the Hypocrites' influence. From what we have said, the picture gradually emerges of a subversive, immoral and dangerous movement. The Hypocrites had no belief in Islam; what then were their motives in joining the Muslim ranks, if not the destruction of Islam from within, seeing that they were too weak to attempt that task openly? This explains, in part, their intimate association with the Jewish opposition in Madina. The Jewish opposition became an open confrontation after the brief initial peace with the Prophet, established by the pact which was to become the written constitution of Madina as a city state. Not only had the Munafiqs a deep and abiding sympathy with the Jewish opposition, but many of their ringleaders were in fact Jews who remained hostile to the Prophet and to Islam, but thought a better job of opposition could be done from within the Islamic ranks. Their designs were aided by the fact that it is very easy for a newcomer to become a Muslim – all he has to do is to declare that he witnesses that there is no God but Allah and that Muhammad is His messenger. Of course, the would-be Muslim has to pretend that he or she is uttering those words with absolute conviction and sincerity. But that is no difficult task for many people.

Some of the ringleaders of the Hypocrites from amongst the Jews were Sa'd ibn Ḥunayf, Zayd ibn al-Luṣayt, Nu'mān ibn Abī Awfā ibn 'Amr, and 'Uthmān ibn 'Awfā. These four belonged to the Jews of Banū Qaynuqā'. Then there was Rafā'ah ibn Zayd ibn al-Tābūt, described by Ibn Hishām as *'kāna kahf al-munāfiqīn'* – i.e. he was an 'enclavement', a hiding-place, for the Munafiqs, providing room and support for their conspiracies. Ibn Hishām narrates that a gale blew when he died. The Prophet was on the way back to Madina – a great gale broke out, making the Muslims most anxious – the Prophet told them that a great unbeliever had died in Madina and this was the reason for the gale.

Another Jewish Hypocrite who offered his house as a secret meeting place for the Munafiqs was al-Suwaylim. This house was later burnt down, on the orders of the Prophet. The activities and manoeuvrings, and the various attitudes the Munafiqs adopted, *vis-à-vis* the Prophet and the Muslims, exposed their sickness of spirit and their evil intentions. They not only waged a campaign of hatred and slander against the Prophet and the Prophet's wives, and against the Muslims in general; they also tried to create disorder and dissension amongst the Muslims. Working secretly, they sought to prevent or sabotage the Muslims' efforts in peace or war. They sided with and aided the Muslims' enemies, and did their best to weaken the Muslims' military lines, every time they were engaged in war. They even attempted to destroy their religious unity and solidarity by building a mosque of dissension (Masjid al-Ḍirār). The climax of their treachery came after the battle of Tabūk, when they attempted to kill the Prophet. From that day on, the Prophet strengthened his war against them. Ḥudhayfah was entrusted with the task of identifying them and of keeping a close watch over their movements. While still observing his own golden rule of 'not letting anyone say that Muhammad kills his own followers', the Prophet did what he could to foil and frustrate their efforts. Finally, he took the decision – to destroy their unity and break up their gangs.

The boycott. Among the various measures adopted against the Munafiqs, there was the eviction from the Prophet's

Mosque of Ibn Ubayy ibn Salūl (see above). After this incident, Ibn Ubayy lost for ever the prestige that, due to the Prophet's courteous tolerance, he had so undeservedly and so long enjoyed. Then, there was the Prophet's order of a social and religious boycott of Rafā'ah ibn Zayd ibn al-Tābūt (the cave of Hypocrites at whose death the wind blew) and of Suwayd ibn al-Ḥārith, because of his mischief and enmity towards the Muslims. Their boycott was commanded by the Qur'ān itself, (al-Mā'idah, 5: 57 and 5: 61). Both men used to make fun of the Prophet and his religion. They used to come to the Prophet saying that they were firm believers in Islam, but Allah exposed their lies and the fact that they used to enter and leave in total unbelief or *Kufr*. The Qur'ān forbade the Muslims to take them as friends, or to show them friendliness or fellow feeling.

The eviction of the Hypocrites from the Prophet's Mosque. Some Hypocrites were in the habit of assembling in the Prophet's Mosque to joke and make fun of all that went on in the mosque. One day, the Prophet entered to find them engaged in their customary behaviour. A group of them were sitting, huddled close together, whispering and laughing. This state of affairs had gone on far too long. The Prophet gave the order that they be immediately thrown out. A mosque is built for worship and piety, not for jesting and hypocrisy. A group of Muslims grabbed them one by one and, forcefully and unceremoniously, threw them out. This incident involved the following Hypocrites: 'Amr ibn Qays; Rāfī' ibn Wadī'ah; Zayd ibn 'Amr (long beard); Qays ibn 'Amr ibn Sahl (the only young man in the group); al-Ḥārith ibn 'Āmir (long-haired man); Suwayd ibn al-Ḥārith. The Munafiqs were violently handled by the Muhajirs. For instance, 'Amr ibn Qays was dragged across the rough floor by one leg and thrown out. Rāfī' ibn Wadī'ah was hit on the face and pulled out of the mosque by his shirt, and told never to approach the Prophet's Mosque again. Zayd ibn 'Amr was pulled along by his long beard and ejected. Also, he was hit rather hard on his chest by 'Umārah ibn Ḥazm, a Companion of the Prophet, and told not to approach the Prophet's Mosque after that day. The only young man in the group (the Hypocrites were generally old men), Qays ibn 'Amr, was prodded in the back of the neck and thus forced outside the mosque. Al-Ḥārith ibn 'Āmir was dragged along the floor of the mosque by his long hair, told that he was *anajas* (unclean spiritually) and warned never to approach the Prophet's Mosque again. And lastly, Suwayd ibn al-Ḥārith was manhandled out of the mosque, told that he was devil-ridden and warned never to enter the mosque again.

The house of Suwaylim the Jew. This house was burnt down just before the Prophet started out on his way to fight the Romans at Tabūk. Making an exception to his own rule never to disclose the destination of his army, the Prophet did disclose it on this occasion, perhaps because of the distance of the march, the harshness of such a road journey in full summer. The Muslims were about to engage the Romans for the first time, who were known to be well-trained in the arts of war, and in no way comparable to the Bedouins of the desert whose tactics were crude and unsophisticated. For this reason, the Prophet disclosed his intention, so that the Muslims might be warned and prepare accordingly.

Quite understandably, there was some reluctance on the part of the feeble-hearted and the Hypocrites to participate in the Tabūk campaign, which was certain to be tough. Some Munafiqs tried very hard to capitalise on the misgivings shown by some faint-hearted Muslims. They fabricated and spread many excuses for those who were afraid to go out to meet the Romans across that very long and arid desert track in the midst of summer. One of the Hypocrites, by the name of al-Jidd ibn Qays, sought the permission of the Prophet not to join the march, simply because, he said, he had a passion for beautiful women and was afraid that if he marched to the Romans, he might become infatuated by their exceptionally beautiful women. The Qur'ān condemned Ibn Qays and rejected his excuse as invalid, saying that he had committed a far greater *fitnah* (sin) than that of being infatuated by beautiful women. Others complained about fighting in the intense heat of the summer and actually sought to discourage Muslims from taking part in the forthcoming fight on this account. This is also reflected in the Qur'ān, which reminds Hypocrites, as well as weak-hearted Muslims, that *Jahannam*

(Hell Fire) is far hotter than the heat of the summer. (al-Tawbah, 9: 81-82)

Now those Hypocrites and others used to assemble in the house of Suwaylim the Jew, who embraced Islam only hypocritically. They were carrying out a well-organised and systematic plan to demoralise the campaign of Tabūk. The Prophet knew of this plan and decided that it could no longer be tolerated. He dispatched a group of Muslims under the command of Ṭalḥah ibn 'Ubayd-Allāh, and ordered them to burn down the house of Suwaylim. The Muslim force proceeded at once and caught the Hypocrites holding one of their meetings. They carried out the Prophet's instructions to the letter. The Hypocrites fled the scene in dismay; however, one of their number, Al Ḍahhāk ibn Khalīfah, chose to make his getaway over the roof and, in so doing, fell and broke his leg.

The mosque of dissension (Masjid al-Ḍirār). In a similar spectacle, the mosque of dissension too was burnt down on the Prophet's orders. The story of this mosque and how it was built is as follows.

A group of Hypocrites, some of whose names we have already mentioned, decided to build a mosque in addition to that of the Prophet's. Their reason was that they needed a mosque because some were disabled, and some were sometimes too busy to make the trip to the Prophet's Mosque in the city centre. Apparently those Hypocrites used to live on the fringes of the city. They said they also needed another mosque for the rainy or cold winter nights. They asked the Prophet, as he was getting ready to leave for Tabūk, to come and pray in their mosque, now that it had been completed. The Prophet apologised, saying that he was too busy then, but promised to visit their mosque after he had returned from the battlefield. But when he was at a place called Zi Awan, to the north of Madina, on the road to Syria, Allah, *subḥānahū wa ta'ālā,* informed His Prophet of the real intentions and motives of those Hypocrites in building the mosque of dissension. Said Allah, *subḥānahū wa ta'ālā,* in the Qur'ān:

> And those who have taken a mosque in opposition and unbelief and to divide the believers and as an outpost for those

> who fought Allah and His Messenger aforetime – they will swear 'We desired nothing but good'; and Allah testifies that they are truly liars.
>
> Never stand therein. A mosque that was founded upon God-fearing from the first day is worthier for you to stand in; therein are men who love to cleanse themselves; and Allah loves those who cleanse themselves. (al-Tawbah, 9: 107, 108)

The Prophet sent two of his Companions, namely Mālik ibn al-Dukhshum and Ma'n ibn 'Udayy and ordered the mosque of dissension to be burnt to the ground. They returned to Madina and immediately carried out their mission. The mosque of dissension was precisely that – it had not been built for the worship of God.

This was the last major, active decision against the Munafiqs. But all the Prophet's measures against them – not least his caution and endurance (he never acted hastily or for mere revenge) – sapped their energy and unity. Truly their cause was an ignoble one, and after the burning down of their mosque, their endeavours were quite ineffective. All thanks are due to Allah.

Part Three

THE MEANING OF THE HIJRA

8

The Islamic Significance of the Hijra

A true Muslim is one whose faith is his highest ideal and highest value, and whose whole life is a struggle to realise this ideal and value. Through that effort, he hopes to earn the favour of God and live freely and with dignity. But there are times and places where it becomes impossible for the Muslim to live as his faith demands – where his freedom and dignity come under pressure or are wholly denied to him. When this happens, both duty and instinct should prompt the Muslim to strive to maintain his *dīn* (religion) and his freedom and dignity. He must fight wholeheartedly against the aggression of injustice and unbelief. Only if fighting is physically impossible, because of a vast imbalance of forces, for instance, does Hijra become an open option. But even then, it does not become an open option unless:

(a) The people to whom the *Dā'iyah* (Caller) of Islam belongs or among whom he lives, are duly called to Islam. Sufficient time must be allowed them in an effort to persuade them to respond to God's call. Judging by the Prophet's stay in Makka, ten to fifteen years are not to be considered too long a time. Nor may this task of spreading the Da'wah, of persuasion, be considered complete, unless every attempt has been made to remove legitimate doubt from the minds of the people concerned and every reasonable challenge answered.

(b) As long as this task remains unaccomplished, mere persecution, even bodily harm, are not a compelling reason for emigration. Nor are hopes of the good life, of more money and more comfort. Only if the Muslims' very lives are in jeopardy is emigration to a new land justifiable. If, for this or a similar reason, some Muslims are compelled to emigrate, a sufficient number – including some leaders – shall remain behind, to carry out the task of persuasion.

TWO ASPECTS OF THE HIJRA

The foregoing ideas are implicit in the concept of the Hijra itself, which is both an historical and a symbolic event. The event as history belongs to Islam's past, but its significance remains with us for all time. Alluding to both these aspects of the Hijra, the Prophet, upon him be peace, said in the Hadith:

> There is no Hijra after the conquest (of Makka), but Jihad (striving in the cause of God) would continue to be obligatory and so would the good intention (to do good deeds). After the conquest of Makka, and if called to make Jihad, obey. (Bukhārī and Muslim)

The Hijra, implied in the latter part of the Hadith, is binding upon Muslims, whenever and wherever conditions of oppression demand it. It is especially binding when Jihad becomes imperative to defend the Muslim community against an aggressor. Hijra would also be obligatory to fulfil the good intentions of gaining knowledge or escaping persecution and oppression.

DĀR AL-ISLĀM AND DĀR AL-ḤARB

According to Muslim jurists, a Muslim must reside only in *Dār al-Islām* (the House of Islam). He must depart from *Dār al-Ḥarb* (a country in which he is in conflict). These two concepts are certainly related to the Hijra both in its historical context and its symbolic meaning. That Muslims are under a religious obligation *not* to reside in Dār al-Ḥarb is maintained by many jurists, who base their ruling on the Qur'ān as well as on the Hadith.

The Qur'ān regards the entire earth as fundamentally the property of God alone, to be shared by the whole human race. To choose one's place of residence is a basic human right, according to Islam. Also, to travel freely, in peace and security, on sea and land, is equally an inalienable human right. It is quite concordant with this thinking that Muslims (or any persons for that matter) should resort to emigration if they find themselves defenceless and helpless in the face of oppression. The Qur'ān strongly condemns any Muslim who fails to avail himself of emigration, should this be required under the conditions indicated above:

> And those whom the angels take (in death), while still doing injustice to themselves, they (the angels) will say: In what were you engaged? They will say: We were oppressed in the land. (The angels) will say: Was not God's earth spacious that you could have migrated therein? As to such men, Hell of Jahannam shall be their abode – an evil destiny ... (al-Nisā', 4: 97)

Al-Qurṭubī, quoting Ibn al-'Arabī, was of the opinion that the Hijra remains obligatory upon Muslims, when the conditions calling for it are fulfilled, until the Day of Resurrection. The Hijra that was terminated was that from Makka to Madina – it was so declared by the Prophet himself, since, after the conquest, Makka itself became Muslim territory. The Hijra which is still valid is that from Dār al-Ḥarb to Dār al-Islām.

What is Dār al-Islām? According to some jurists, Dār al-Islām is a country or a territory in which the law of Islam (the Shari'ah) rules supremely. No law should be allowed to override it. Needless to say, in Dār al-Islām an environment must be striven after that promotes the security and well-being of Muslims; where Muslims may live in peace, freedom and dignity, and perform their religious rites and duties without impediment of any sort. In Dār al-Islām a Muslim must be confident of justice and equality and be encouraged to develop his powers and realise his aspirations. Above all, Dār al-Islām means a society whose central commitment is to uphold the ideals of Islam, to foster and persevere in God's grand design for man on this earth. Dār al-Islām is thus the home of the Muslim Umma, custodians of all humanity of the true faith.

Dār al-Ḥarb. Dār al-Ḥarb is any country or territory which cannot be called Dār al-Islām. It is a place in which (1) the law of Islam (the Shari'ah) is not enforced in a paramount way; and (2) the religious and human rights of Muslims are not safeguarded or promoted or protected, but, on the contrary, violated and undermined.

The Muslim is naturally averse to Dār al-Ḥarb and ought to put himself in conflict and at war with it. If he fails to transform it into a Dār al-Islām, and if he is prevented from working towards such a transformation, then his second best option is to migrate to a new land and seek another, better environment.

In particular, he is under a strong religious obligation to migrate to a Dār al-Islām, if there be one. We should recall, in this connection, that Dār al-Islām is a society open to all Muslims regardless of their ethnic or linguistic background – a country or territory to which every Muslim on the globe has a claim, especially if that Muslim is compelled to leave his own land because of oppression or persecution against which he is defenceless and helpless. Of course, this helplessness must be judged to be genuine, not merely some form of cowardice, defeatism or escapism in the face of hardship and struggle.

Another view of Dār al-Islām and Dār al-Ḥarb. The foregoing view on the distinction between Dār al-Islām and Dār al-Ḥarb is too hard and fast, according to a second and more moderate view. There are important graduations within Dār al-Islām itself, according to the degree of its commitment to Islam.

(a) *Dār al-'Adl* (land of justice), where Islamic law is fully enforced and rules supremely. Muslims are secure and are able to live according to the Islamic ideals in justice and peace. Muslims are advised to live in it and migrate to it.

(b) *Dār al-Baghy* (land of usurption). This is a Muslim land in which an illegitimate authority has been set up and the legitimate Muslim ruler is forcefully removed or overthrown. Muslims are obliged to resist the illegitimate authority and to strive for the restoration of the legitimate authority.

(c) *Dār al-Bid'ah* (place of misguided innovations), where innovations unsanctioned by Islam are widespread, where the Sunnah of the Prophet is ignored or not given its rightful place. The duty of the Muslims here is to fight the spread of un-Islamic innovations and work towards the complete implementation of the Sunnah.

(d) *Al-Dār al-Maslūbah.* This is a country or territory that was once a Muslim land, inhabited by Muslims and ruled by the Islamic law, but has since been usurped and occupied by the enemies of Islam. It is a religious obligation for every Muslim to wage legitimate war to regain it and drive out the usurpers and colonisers. The duty of liberating this usurped land lies with every Muslim, not just those Muslims who have been subjected to the occupation.

These four categories are all included in Dār al-Islām – according to the second, moderate view. In all, the Muslim's duty is to stand and fight, and not to resort to Hijra except in the very last eventuality.

A third view of Dār al-Islām and Dār al-Ḥarb which is even more moderate than the second view, is attributed to Abū Ḥanīfah. According to Abū Ḥanīfah, a country or a territory becomes a Dār al-Islām if it satisfies two conditions: (a) the Muslims must be able to enjoy peace and security; and (b) it must have common frontiers with some Muslim countries (other places of Dār al-Islām). This view, which makes no reference to the supreme rule of Islamic law, allows greater freedom of movement to, and residence in, places around the world, so long as these are not too far from the heart of the Islamic world. Probably the second condition is intended to offer the possibility of a safe retreat in the eventuality that Muslims are, unexpectedly, subjected to hardship or persecution. The common boundary with an orthodox Dār al-Islām will make it possible for a Muslim government to intervene on their behalf. According to this third view, then, Muslims can take residence in such proximate lands, so long as they can earn their living in peace and practise their religious duties without affront to their dignity.

A contemporary version of Abū Ḥanīfah's view can be envisaged by extending the concept of proximity, which is for him, quite understandably, exclusively territorial. Given the revolution in communications, proximity becomes increasingly relative. 'Accessibility' may be a more relevant term for modern times. The more open a society is in allowing free movement of its residents across its national frontiers, the more 'accessible' it is. Muslims should, then, be able to move out of their country of residence (where they formerly enjoyed peace and security) to another place, possibly to a Dār al-Islām, in which not only security is guaranteed, but also the Islamic law rules supreme. Having said this, it is again interesting to speculate whether it really was in Abū Ḥanīfah's mind that common boundaries would permit Muslims to cross over to a Dār al-Islām in case of oppression?

However that may be, Abū Ḥanīfah's view has important consequences for the position of Muslim minorities the world over. His definition of Dār al-Islām would encourage them – so long as, of course, their security is not endangered – to adopt a more constructive and vigorous attitude to residing in countries whose dominant culture is non-Islamic. Islam is, after all, a universalist religion, recognising no boundaries of race or language. The earth as a whole belongs to God, and Muslims have an important message to convey to mankind – it is their privilege to be trustees of this universal mission. Abū Ḥanīfah's view, permitting greater movement, encourages at one and the same time a spirit of wonder and exploration and a desire to communicate the ideals of Islam.

Implicit in the foregoing discussion has been the principle that Hijra – even in its broader, symbolic sense – is not to be undertaken for worldly reasons. This does not mean that Islam prohibits travel and emigration for the purposes of earning money, of increasing knowledge, or even simply of tourism – on the contrary, the Qur'ān directs Muslims to undertake such travels whenever it is fruitful to do so. But such travels or emigrations should not be given the distinguished epithet of 'Hijra'. Hijra, whether large or small numbers of people are involved, must, strictly speaking, have as its central motive a genuinely God-inspired goal.

FURTHER IMPLICATIONS OF THE HIJRA

So far we have conducted our discussion on the necessity of Hijra in order to (a) escape oppression and persecution; when the Hijra is an emigration to a place where the Muslim can live in peace and security; and (b) in order to set up a Muslim authority within a Muslim land where only God is worshipped and religion becomes God's alone. However, there is another issue for which Hijra becomes a binding duty upon every Muslim capable of undertaking it. The Qur'ān states that Muslims everywhere are brethren and protectors of each other. Therefore, should any group of Muslims anywhere in the world be subjected to aggression or oppression, then it is an obligation upon other Muslims to come to their aid, even if they live outside the Muslim territory. Qur'ānic verses to this effect are:

> And the believers, men and women, are protecting allies one

> of the other, they enjoin righteousness and they forbid evil; they establish prayer and pay *Zakāt*. (al-Tawbah, 9: 71)
>
> How is it with you, that you do not fight in the way of God, and for the oppressed among men, women and children who say, 'Oh our Lord, bring us forth from this city whose people (oppress us) and appoint for us a protector from Thee and appoint for us from Thee a helper. (al-Nisā', 4: 75)

When setting out to defend the weak and the oppressed, the Muslim should give priority to those nearest to him in location. The Qur'ān seems to state this priority as follows:

> O you who believe! Fight the unbelievers who are near to you, and let them find in you a harshness and know that God is with the God-fearing. (al-Tawbah, 9: 123)

Finally, Hijra is also called for to spread the message and teaching of Islam in lands it has not reached. This duty supercedes even the duty to answer the call for Jihad, in the case of those few learned Muslims who have the ability to discharge it. In the formative years of Islam, the Prophet sent out many learned men, even in the face of great perils, to teach the Qur'ān. Many of those early teachers lost their lives in the cause of spreading the call of Islam.

9

The Political Implications of the Hijra

At the beginning of the fifteenth century of Hijra, we consider afresh the importance and value of the Hijra[1] in the political history of Islam. Everyone agrees that the Hijra ushered in the beginning of the first civilisation of Islam. However, there seems to be precious little appreciation of the primarily ideological and political significance of that event in the establishment of the Islamic society. In what follows, we attempt to expose the shortcomings of some current interpretations of the Hijra, and advance (hopefully) more satisfactory ones that do justice to this most crucial event in the evolution of early Muslim society and subsequent Muslim history.

WHAT THE HIJRA IS NOT

Let us begin with two current interpretations of the Hijra which, in our view, fall far short of giving it its rightful place in the formative history of Islam. The first interpretation is the *flight* interpretation. The second is the *arbitration* interpretation. Both are unknown in Muslim sources. They have been adopted, and introduced into Muslim thought, by Western and Orientalist scholars.

The flight interpretation represents the Hijra as a flight from the Makkan crucible – as a running away, so to speak, from persecution by the polytheists of Makka. Early Western accounts of the Hijra, almost all, systematically use the term 'flight' to describe the Prophet's Hijra from Makka to Madina. In view of the obvious unambiguous connotation of the Arabic word 'Hijra' (the straightforward literal English rendering of which is 'emigration') one cannot but wonder why Orientalists

[1] The Hijra referred to here is the historical one of the Prophet and his Companions from Makka to Yathrib.

have preferred to use the word 'flight' instead. Given good faith, the negative connotation of the word 'flight' should have deterred anyone, seeking to elucidate the true significance of the Hijra, from using it. Any implication that the Hijra was in fact a *withdrawal* from the ideological war that raged in Makka, between nascent Islam and its pagan adversaries, is, from the account we have given above, a gross misinterpretation.

More substantial than the flight theory is the arbitration theory. According to this, Yathrib (Madina) was going through a period characterised by anarchy and conflict. The two leading tribes of Aws and Khazraj were on the brink of open warfare over the control of the city. The Jewish settlers there seemed to have failed in their efforts to mediate between the two warring tribes, and it is not far-fetched to suggest that they might even have contributed, in some measure, to the perpetuation of the conflict. Such a perpetuation would have given them the privileged status of playing the roles of judges and arbitrators each time there was a fresh outbreak of hostilities.

According to the theory, the Yathribites invited the Prophet to come to Madina because they were weary of the continuing wars and hostilities. They wanted him to act as arbitrator in the age-long dispute between Aws and Khazraj. They were quite ready to accept the implications of the role they were offering the Prophet. Most important among these implications was the acceptance of the Prophet's authority over the city of Yathrib.

It is our contention that, substantial and intelligent as it is, the arbitration theory does not do justice to the full meaning of the Hijra. Evidence from the *Sīrah* of Ibn Hishām depicting the events of the Second Pledge of 'Aqaba sufficiently refutes, we believe, the main point of the arbitration theory – that the Yathribites grew weary of the war amongst themselves and urgently needed an arbitrator. Firstly, the second pledge has been termed the *Pledge of War* by all the Muslim biographers of the Prophet. The reason for this is that it contained a commitment, notably absent from the first 'Aqaba pledge, to fight, should that become necessary for the defence and safety of the Prophet himself, or his followers, once they arrived in

Madina. By contrast, the first 'Aqaba pledge was called the *Pledge of Women* because it was mainly a pledge to abide by the moral standards and religious rules and obligations of Islam, the kind of commitments women have to make when they accept Islam. There was no mention of fighting in the first 'Aqaba pledge.

Rather than being in search of an arbitrator, the Yathribites were, in fact, seeking the Prophet with the Divine mission whose appearance was foretold by the people with Scripture living in Yathrib. In particular, the Jews of Yathrib were anxiously awaiting his coming. Secondly, the terms of the second 'Aqaba pledge leave little doubt as to the attitude of those leaders of Aws and Khazraj who accepted them. Ibn Hishām, quoting Ibn Isḥāq, has given the following account:

> Ibn Isḥāq said: The Pledge of War took place after God had given permission to His Messenger, upon him be peace, to wage war. It comprised conditions other than those which he [the Prophet] had laid down in the first 'Aqaba Pledge. The first pledge was in the manner of the Pledge of Women because God had not then given permission to His Messenger, upon him be peace, to wage war. When God gave permission to wage it, and the Messenger of God, upon him be peace, then took the pledge in the last 'Aqaba for waging war on any of his persecutors [*lit.* on people be they red or black] he took conditions for himself [i.e. for his protection] and took further conditions from those people for [obedience to] his Lord. He made Paradise the reward for the keeping and fulfilling of that pledge.
>
> Ibn Isḥāq said: I have been told by 'Ubādah ibn al-Walīd ibn 'Ubādah ibn al-Sāmit on the authority of his father al-Walīd, on the authority of his grandfather 'Ubādah ibn al-Sāmit, who was one of the *Nuqabā'* [deputies], that: The Messenger of God, upon him be peace, has taken from us the Pledge of War. 'Ubādah was one of the Twelve *Nuqabā'* who had taken the 'Pledge of Women' at the first 'Aqaba that we obey the Prophet in times of hardship and times of ease, (to fulfil any undertaking irrespective of whether we like or hate it, even against our self-interest). We shall not contest the authority of those in charge, and we say the truth wherever we are, not fearing when obeying God, the censure of anyone.

Further evidence that the Aws and Khazraj tribes of Yathrib

were committing themselves to fight in defence of the Prophet and the oppressed Muslims of Makka is provided by a statement made by one of their leaders, namely al-'Abbās ibn Ubādah ibn Naḍlah al-Anṣārī. During the enactment of the second 'Aqaba pledge, when the Yathribite delegation of eighty-three men and women were about to enter the phase of handshaking (an act signalling official conclusion of the pledge), he reminded everyone that they were giving a solemn pledge to wage war against whoever happened to oppose the Prophet, 'be they red or black'; and that if they doubted their ability to honour the pledge when their lives were endangered or their money or property threatened, then they should be wise enough not to make it. However, the delegation was wholeheartedly adamant in its determination both to make and to honour that commitment at any cost, whether to their lives or their property. They then went on to give a reassuring demonstration of their resolve to honour the defence pact. As soon as the handshaking was completed, they asked permission of the Prophet to make a raid against the Quraysh, the chief oppressors of the Muslims. But the Prophet calmed them, saying that he had not as yet received any order or permission to wage war.

This refutes conclusively, in our view, the arbitration theory proposed by a leading Orientalist. Far from being either a flight or a retreat, the Hijra, and the Pledge that made it possible, firmly ushered in the beginning of a positive and effective stage in the process of inviting the people to Islam and establishing the first Muslim civilisation. It provided a point of departure in the life of the early Muslims, who, for thirteen years, had been commanded by the Prophet not to retaliate against their persecutors and oppressors, but rather to endure patiently and courageously the indignities which the ignorant and, ultimately, ineffective polytheists of Makka were wont to heap upon them. From the Hijra onwards the Muslims were granted permission to fight in self-defence. They were permitted to wage war to liberate themselves and purge their land from the unseemly and unjust practices of the polytheists who transgressed against them and caused them physical and moral suffering. The transformation from the passive to the active stage was only made possible by the resolved will of the Yathribites, leaders of the Aws and Khazraj, to wage war on behalf of the Prophet and his oppressed followers. Thus it is totally implausible to suggest that the Yathribites invited the Prophet to come to Madina because they needed someone who would end the dispute in which they were involved.

THE POSITIVE SIGNIFICANCE OF THE HIJRA

It is interesting to speculate about the wisdom of restraining the Muslims from fighting, even in self-defence, throughout the Makkan period. Perhaps it was important that their character, their fortitude and forbearance in the cause of Islam, should be severely tested. Probably it was futile to fight when they did not possess the necessary force, in numbers or arms, to wage a successful war. Perhaps it was that Islam needed a period of time in which to establish itself peacefully and on the merit of its own intrinsic spiritual and moral strength, without the further support of military force. Whatever the reasons that led to the absolute prohibition of fighting which the Prophet imposed on his early, much-oppressed followers, the situation was dramatically changed as soon as the Muslims managed to secure a political and military presence in the territory of Yathrib by the voluntary consent of the vast majority of its population.

Only after Yathrib had been secured as a base upon which a Muslim authority could be set up, was it possible for Muslim civilisation to take root and expand. If we are to draw the moral from the Hijra, if we wish to be guided by its positive implications, then we must reflect adequately and at length upon the conditions and imperatives which made possible the first Muslim society, the first Muslim civilisation in Madina.

THE TERRITORIAL IMPERATIVE

Islam is not only a body of ideals and doctrines, but a practical system of politics and laws. As such it seeks to realise in practice its model of society, state and civilisation. Now, no society, state or civilisation can be formed without a territorial base. So long as the Muslims remained without a secure and defensible territory, they could not realistically hope to obtain or defend their human rights. So long as they remained residents of a non-Muslim land they could not aspire to the achievement of their ideals, nor even live with honour and justice. Thus, the securing of a self-sufficient and defensible land becomes the first imperative in the way of forming a Muslim civilisation.

The Prophet must have understood, through Divine revelation, and must consequently have deemed futile any attempt to exhaust the Muslims' energies or sacrifice their lives in a fruitless armed struggle within the framework of the Makkan society. If the Muslims had embarked upon a course of violent confrontation with the Makkan polytheists, they might have been utterly destroyed and their religion with them. Passive resistance was the best policy for survival when a small group of peaceful, unarmed men found themselves face to face with the unlimited, unchecked power of an evil and immoral state.

THE IDEOLOGICAL IMPERATIVE

A Muslim civilisation is one founded on the principles and articles of Islam and rooted in the bonds of religious fraternity of the Muslim community. For this reason, a Muslim society is ideological and the basis for belonging to it is a commitment to the common feelings, beliefs and convictions of the people rightly included in it. The essence of the fundamental transformation which the new-born Islam was able to bring to the Arabian society lay in its substitution of this ideological basis for the blood *'Aṣābiyyah* of *Jāhiliyyah* (pagan-barbaric) times. The Muslim society is thus an open society, ready to include and embrace anyone willing to belong to it. Belonging to it means nothing more or less than having a willingness and a commitment to abide by its rules. The widening human, egalitarian horizons which Islam opens up in this respect are quite unmatched. If we ponder but for a moment on the barriers that divide the human race in the contemporary world, then we are – as Muslims – justified in feeling a sense of gratitude and satisfaction in the progressive and liberalising tendency of Islam.

Human societies today are based either on narrow nationalistic or often false patriotic sentiments. There are even some societies that are based on blatant racialism or have strong cultural biases exclusive and inhuman in their norms and ideals. Communist societies are based upon an ideology which denies and undermines most of what is characteristically human in us and rejects totally any Divine or spiritual quality of life. Capitalist societies are so much geared towards material self-interest that the liberties they acclaim are often empty and hollow.

Islamic civilisation in Yathrib was only based upon ideological commitment – a commitment that was as broad and open as it was human in scope. The ideological society could not have existed without a territory. Nor would it have been possible had it not been for the supreme and unchallenged political authority that Muslims enjoyed in Madina.

POLITICAL AUTHORITY

The third imperative is therefore that of political authority and political control. Islam is not like any other religion because it lays clear and unambiguous claim to government. It has a political theory as well as a positive law of its own. Without the materialisation of its political theory and the enforcement of its positive law, the Islamic community cannot and will not be in a position to thrive and prosper, nor uphold its characteristic sociological features, norms and values. The Prophet clearly recognised the vitality of the state and the political authority of a truly Muslim environment and society. Because of this, he explicitly demanded, and obtained, the acceptance of his personal authority in his capacity as Messenger of God over the city of Yathrib. This demand was explicitly mentioned as one of the conditions of the second 'Aqaba Pledge, and the Yathribites explicitly assented to it by declaring their intention and firm commitment not to contest the authority of the new administration which they were by contract, conscious desire and explicit pledge, inviting to their own city. And they made this solemn pledge without any motive of self-interest or in any hope of some 'return' for political support.

These three imperatives – territorial, the ideological and political control – are the necessary conditions for the establishment of a Muslim community. Without their realisation, the Muslim cannot rightly entertain any hopes of *falāḥ* (well-being).

THE MOBILISATION OF THE MUSLIM CHARACTER

The establishment of the Muslim community could not have been carried out without the personal effort and commitment of the individual Muslim. The human element was, and is, and always will be, one of the most essential factors in any historical change. It was therefore important that the Muslim character should be raised to the highest level of commitment and competence in pursuit of the ideals of Islam. The task of building up a strong, reflective Muslim personality is very great indeed, and that of realising the dreams and values of a conscious Muslim personality is even greater – because in the second stage of establishing a Muslim civilisation, the Muslims have to contend with contrary forces and contrary interests. But the two responsibilities interpenetrate: strife against the inner urges of the self in a sense is continued in the strife against the more tangible, aggressive, external forces. The Muslim character is put to the test when, while upholding faith within, it must face exacting demands from without. The time of persecution in Makka was, equally with the active Madina phase, just such a putting to the test.

A revolutionising process is essential to bring about a new awareness in the individual consciousness – an awareness that will enable him to understand that his personal dignity and honour, as well as his personal safety, are at stake should he fail to create the society and the state in which he can expect to live in honourable peace and security. He should not expect to declare his ideals as a Muslim and live by them in a non-Muslim society without that society attempting to encroach on, to limit, his rights.

But the new awareness of himself as a Muslim is needed also to shake the individual free of false identities, and false hopes that he may be accepted as a full Muslim in a non-Muslim society. It is important that all such hopes of belonging to non-Muslim communities, of being accepted by them with honour and justice and equality, should be shed and exposed as mere fantasies. Non-Muslim societies will never accept nor enable a truly conscious Muslim – a Muslim who is aware of his full identity as Muslim – to realise the ideals of Islam. His attitude and behaviour will be bound to evoke feelings of aversion and outright enmity from persons who are confirmed citizens of the non-Muslim society. The only way for him to achieve some kind of quick peace or acceptance in such a society is to compromise his beliefs or to be hypocritical, developing in the process an inferiority complex *vis-à-vis* the dominant non-Muslim society.

The only way to avoid these wretched consequences is to challenge the sterile communities and cultures that refuse to heed the Divine call of Islam. Here it is important to shake away false spatio-temporal identities – identities with a certain place and with the present in which it expresses itself. The Muslim must, as part of the revolutionising process, be emancipated from the here-and-now requirements of the material environment. He must aspire to a more fertile, more receptive, more sympathetic and generous, a much broader, set of here-and-nows. It is perhaps with this in mind that most Muslim authorities have labelled all non-Muslim environments Dār al-Ḥarb as distinct from Dār al-Islām. It was perhaps also with this intent that the Prophet was explicitly commanded by the Qur'ān not to extend protection or social responsibilities to those who failed to make the Hijra and thus failed to appreciate the importance of *earning* the protection of the Muslim government through the emancipating, but sacrifice-demanding process of the Hijra.

In our contemporary efforts to recreate a Muslim civilisation which will satisfy our aspirations and realise our vision of a just society which is both Divinely-guided and sensitive to the plight of the modern man, we must give thought to the political implications of the Hijra. It provides a living, historical example of what is possible in the greatest adversity, and a living symbol and ideal of what is desirable, both for the individual Muslim and for the Muslim state.

Index